HOW PROUST CAN
CHANGE YOUR LIFE

'In all [de Botton's] books serious philosophical ideas,
teasing advice for lovers and thoughts on literature are
tossed in the air and spun together like juggling balls.
The display is so dazzling that you almost don't notice
how clever de Botton is actually being. It is this sleight
of hand which places him squarely in the finest,
and most witty, tradition of European writing'
CRESSIDA CONNOLLY, *Sunday Express*

'I was fascinated by his approach to literature
in general – it is a sort of Proust as Bible and I think
the wisdom of Proust is very well accentuated'
MURIEL SPARK

'A pleasure to cherish'
MICHÈLE ROBERTS

'Marvellous'
RICHARD KLEIN, *Village Voice*

'The funniest book I've read in ages'
ANDREW MARR, *Independent*

ALAIN DE BOTTON is the author of ten
bestselling books including *The Consolations of Philosophy*
and *The Art of Travel*. He was born in 1969
and lives in London.

For more information, consult:
www.alaindebotton.com

Alain de Botton

How Proust
Can Change
Your Life

PICADOR

First published 1997 by Picador

First published in paperback 1998 by Picador
an imprint of Pan Macmillan, a division of Macmillan Publishers Limited
Pan Macmillan, 20 New Wharf Road, London N1 9RR
Basingstoke and Oxford
Associated companies throughout the world
www.panmacmillan.com

ISBN 978-0-330-35491-2

A CIP catalogue record for this book is available from
the British Library.

Typeset by SetSystems Limited, Saffron Walden
Printed and bound by CPI Group (UK) Ltd, Croydon, CR0 4YY

Contents

CHAPTER ONE

How to Love
Life Today

There are few things humans are more dedicated to than unhappiness. Had we been placed on earth by a malign creator for the exclusive purpose of suffering, we would have good reason to congratulate ourselves on our enthusiastic response to the task. Reasons to be inconsolable abound: the frailty of our bodies, the fickleness of love, the insincerities of social life, the compromises of friendship, the deadening effects of habit. In the face of such persistent ills, we might naturally expect that no event would be awaited with greater anticipation than the moment of our own extinction.

Someone looking for a paper to read in Paris in the 1920s might have picked up a title called *L'Intransigeant*. It had a reputation for investigative news, metropolitan gossip, comprehensive classifieds and incisive editorials. It also had a habit of dreaming up big questions and asking French celebrities to send in their replies. 'What do you think would be the ideal education to give your daughter?' was one. 'Do you have any recommendations for improving traffic congestion in Paris?' was another. In the summer of 1922, the paper formulated a particularly elaborate question for its contributors.

An American scientist announces that the world will end, or at least that such a huge part of the continent will be destroyed, and in such a sudden way, that death will be the certain fate of hundreds of millions of people. If this prediction were confirmed, what do you think would be its effects on people between the time when they acquired the aforementioned certainty and the moment of cataclysm? Finally, as far as you're concerned, what would you do in this last hour?

The first celebrity to respond to the grim scenario of personal and global annihilation was a then distinguished, now forgotten man of letters named Henri Bordeaux, who suggested that it would drive the mass of the population directly into either the nearest church or the nearest bedroom, though he himself avoided the awkward choice, explaining that he would take this last opportunity to climb a mountain, so as to admire the beauty of Alpine scenery and flora. Another Parisian celebrity, an accomplished actress called Berthe Bovy, proposed no recreations of her own, but shared with her readers a coy concern that men would shed all inhibitions once their actions had ceased to carry long-term consequences. This dark prognosis matched that of a famous Parisian palm reader, Madame Fraya, who judged that people would omit to spend their last hours contemplating the extraterrestrial future and would be too taken up with worldly pleasures to give much thought to readying their souls for the afterlife – a suspicion confirmed when another writer, Henri Robert, blithely declared his intention to devote himself to a final game of bridge, tennis and golf.

The last celebrity to be consulted on his pre-apocalypse plans was a reclusive, moustachioed novelist not known for his interest in golf, tennis or bridge [though he had once tried draughts, and twice aided in the launching of a kite], a man who had spent the last fourteen years lying in a narrow bed under a pile of thinly woven woollen blankets writing an unusually long novel without an adequate bedside lamp. Since the publication of its first volume in 1913, *In Search of Lost Time* had been hailed as a masterpiece, a French reviewer had compared the author to Shakespeare, an Italian critic had likened him to Stendhal and an Austrian princess had offered her hand in marriage. Though he had never esteemed himself highly ['If only I could value myself more! Alas! It is impossible'] and had once referred to himself as a flea and to his writing as a piece of indigestible nougat, Marcel Proust had grounds for satisfaction. Even the British ambassador to France, a man of wide acquaintance and cautious judgement, had deemed it appropriate to bestow on him a great, if not directly literary honour, describing him as, 'The most remarkable man I have ever met – because he keeps his overcoat on at dinner.'

Enthusiastic about contributing to newspapers, and in any case a good sport, Proust sent the following reply to *L'Intransigeant* and its catastrophic American scientist:

> I think that life would suddenly seem wonderful to us if we were threatened to die as you say. Just think of how

many projects, travels, love affairs, studies it – our life – hides from us, made invisible by our laziness which, certain of a future, delays them incessantly.

But let all this threaten to become impossible for ever, how beautiful it would become again! Ah! if only the cataclysm doesn't happen this time, we won't miss visiting the new galleries of the Louvre, throwing ourselves at the feet of Miss X., making a trip to India.

The cataclysm doesn't happen, we don't do any of it, because we find ourselves back in the heart of normal life, where negligence deadens desire. And yet we shouldn't have needed the cataclysm to love life today. It would have been enough to think that we are humans, and that death may come this evening.

Feeling suddenly attached to life when we realize the imminence of death suggests that it was perhaps not life itself which we had lost the taste for so long as there was no end in sight, but our quotidian version of it, that our dissatisfactions were more the result of a certain way of living than of anything irrevocably morose about human experience. Having surrendered the customary belief in our own immortality, we would then be reminded of a host of untried possibilities lurking beneath the surface of an apparently undesirable, apparently eternal existence.

However, if due acknowledgement of our mortality encourages us to re-evaluate our priorities, we may well ask what these priorities should be. We might only have been living half a life before we faced up to the implications of death, but what exactly does a whole life consist of? Simple recognition of our inevitable demise does not guarantee that we will latch on to any sensible answers when it comes to filling in what remains of the diary. Panicked by the ticking of the clock, we may even resort to some spectacular follies. The suggestions sent by the Parisian celebrities to *L'Intransigeant* were contradictory enough: admiration of Alpine scenery, contemplation of the extraterrestrial future, tennis, golf. But were any of these fruitful ways to pass the time before the continent disintegrated?

Proust's own suggestions [Louvre, love, India] were no more helpful. For a start, they were at odds with what one knows of his character. He had never been an avid museum visitor, he hadn't been to the Louvre for over a decade, and preferred to look at reproductions than face the chatter of a museum crowd ['People think the love of literature, painting and music has become extremely widespread, whereas there isn't a single person who knows anything about them']. Nor was he known for his interest in the Indian subcontinent, which was a trial to reach, requiring a train down to Marseilles, a mailboat to Port Said and ten days on a P&O liner across the Arabian Sea, hardly an ideal itinerary for a man with difficulty stepping out of bed. As for Miss X, to his mother's distress, Marcel had never proved receptive to her charms, nor to those of the Misses A to Z; and it was a long time since he had bothered to ask if there was a younger brother at hand, having concluded that a glass of well-chilled beer offered a more reliable source of pleasure than lovemaking.

But even if he had wanted to act according to his proposals, Proust turned out to have had little chance. Only four months after sending his answer to *L'Intransigeant*, having predicted that something like this would happen for years, he caught a cold and died. He was fifty-one. He had been invited to a party and, despite the symptoms of a mild flu, he wrapped himself in three coats and two blankets and went out all the same. On his way home, he had to wait in a glacial courtyard for a taxi, and there caught a chill. It developed into a high fever which might have been contained, if Proust hadn't refused to take the advice of doctors summoned to his bedside. Fearing that they would disrupt his work, he turned down their offer of camphorated oil injections, and continued to write, failing to eat or drink anything besides hot milk, coffee and stewed fruit. The cold turned into a bronchitis, which snowballed into a pneumonia. Hopes of recovery were briefly raised when he sat up in bed and requested a grilled sole, but by the time the fish was bought and cooked he was seized by nausea and was unable to touch it. He died a few hours later from a burst abscess in his lung.

Fortunately, Proust's reflections on how to live were not limited to an all too brief and somewhat confusing reply to a fanciful question from a newspaper – because, right up to his death, he had been at work on a book which set out to answer, albeit in a rather extended and narratively complex form, a question not dissimilar to the one provoked by the predictions of the fictional American scientist.

The title of the long book hinted as much. Though Proust never liked it, and referred to it variously as 'unfortunate' [1914], 'misleading' [1915] and 'ugly' [1917], *In Search of Lost Time* had the advantage of pointing directly enough to a central theme of the novel: a search for the causes behind the dissipation and loss of time. Far from a memoir tracing the passage of a more lyrical age, it was a practical, universally applicable story about how to stop wasting, and begin appreciating one's life.

Though the announcement of an imminent apocalypse could no doubt make this a concern uppermost in anyone's mind, the Proustian guidebook held out a hope that the topic could detain us a little before personal or global destruction was at hand; and that we might therefore learn to adjust our priorities before it was time to have a last game of golf and keel over.

CHAPTER TWO

HOW TO READ
FOR YOURSELF

Proust was born into a family where the art of making people feel better was taken very seriously indeed. His father was a doctor, a vast, bearded man with a characteristic nineteenth-century physiognomy, who had the authoritative air and purposeful glance that might readily have made one feel a sissy. He exuded the moral superiority available to the medical profession, a group whose value to society is unquestionably apparent to anyone who has ever suffered from a tickly cough or ruptured appendix, and which may hence provoke an uncomfortable sense of superfluity in those with less certifiably worthwhile vocations.

Dr Adrien Proust had started modestly, the son of a provincial grocer specializing in the manufacture of wax candles for the home and church. After pursuing brilliant medical studies, culminating in a thesis on *The Different Forms of Softening of the Brain*, Dr Proust had devoted himself to improving standards of public sanitation. He was especially concerned with arresting the spread of cholera and bubonic plague, and had travelled widely outside France, advising foreign governments on infectious diseases. He was appropriately rewarded for his efforts, becoming a Chevalier de la Légion d'Honneur and a professor of hygiene at the Medical Faculty in Paris. The mayor of the once cholera-prone port of Toulon presented him with the keys to the city and a hospital for quarantined victims was named after him in Marseilles. By the time of his death in 1903, Adrien Proust was a doctor of international standing, who could almost be believed when he summed up his existence with the thought, 'I have been happy all my life.'

No wonder Marcel should have felt somewhat unworthy next to his father, and feared that he had been the bane of this contented life. He had never harboured any of the professional aspirations which constituted a badge of normality in a late-nineteenth-century bourgeois household. Literature was the only thing he cared for, though did not, for much of his youth, seem too willing, or able, to write. Because he was a good son, he tried at first to do something his parents would approve of. There were thoughts of joining the Foreign Ministry, of becoming a lawyer, a stockbroker or an assistant at the Louvre. Yet the hunt for a career proved difficult. Two weeks of work experience with a solicitor horrified him ['In my most desperate moments, I have never conceived of anything more horrible than a law office'], and the idea of becoming a diplomat was ruled out when he realized it would involve moving away from Paris and his beloved mother. 'What is there left, given that I have decided to become neither a lawyer, nor a doctor, nor a priest . . . ?' asked an increasingly desperate twenty-two-year-old Proust.

Perhaps he could become a librarian. He applied and was chosen for an unpaid post at the Mazarine Library. It might have been the answer, but Proust found the place too dusty for his lungs and asked for an ever-longer series of sick leaves, some of which he spent in bed, others on holiday, but few at a writing desk. He led an apparently charmed life, organizing dinner parties, going out for tea and spending money like water. One can imagine the distress of his father, a practical man who had never displayed much interest in the arts [though he had once served in the Medical corps of the Opéra Comique and had charmed an American opera singer, who sent him a picture of herself dressed as a man in frilly knee-length pantaloons]. After repeatedly failing to report for work, showing up one day a year or less, even Marcel's unusually tolerant library employers finally lost their patience and dismissed him five years after he had first been taken on. It had by this time become evident to all, not least his disappointed father, that Marcel would never have a proper job – and would remain forever reliant on family money to pursue his unremunerative and dilettantish interest in literature.

Which could make it hard to understand an ambition Proust confided to his maid once both his parents had died, and he had finally started work on his novel.

'Ah, Céleste,' he said, 'if I could be sure of doing with my books as much as my father did for the sick.'

To do with books what Adrien had done for those ravaged by cholera and bubonic plague? One didn't have to be the mayor of Toulon to realize that Dr Proust had it in his power to effect an improvement in people's condition, but what sort of healing did Marcel have in mind with the seven volumes of *In Search of Lost Time?* The opus might be a way to pass a slow-moving train journey across the Siberian steppes, but would one wish to claim that its benefits matched those of a properly functioning public sanitation system?

If we dismiss Marcel's ambitions, it may have more to do with a particular scepticism towards the therapeutic qualities of the literary novel than with all-encompassing doubts as to the value of the printed word. Even Dr Proust, in many ways unsympathetic to his son's vocation, was not hostile towards every published genre, and indeed, turns out to have been a prolific author himself, for a long time far better known in the bookshops than his offspring.

However, unlike his son's, the utility of Dr Proust's writings was never in question. Across an output of thirty-four books, he devoted himself to considering a multitude of ways in which to further the physical well-being of the population, his titles ranging from a study of *The Defence of Europe Against the Plague* to a slim volume on the specialized and, at the time, novel problem of *Saturnism as Observed in Workers Involved in the Making of Electric Batteries.* But Dr Proust was perhaps best known among the reading public for a number of books conveying in concise, lively and accessible language all that one might wish to know about physical fitness. It would in no way have contravened the tenor of his ambitions to have described him as a pioneer and master of the keep-fit self-help manual.

His most successful self-help book was entitled *Elements of Hygiene*; it was published in 1888, was fully illustrated and was aimed at teenage girls, who were deemed to need advice on enhancing their health in order to produce a vigorous new generation of French citizens, of whom there was a shortfall after a century of bloody military adventures.

With interest in a healthy lifestyle having only increased since Dr Proust's day, there may be value in including at least a few of the doctor's many insightful recommendations.

How Dr Proust Can Change Your Health

(i) Backache
Almost always down to incorrect posture. When a teenage girl is sewing, she must take care not to lean forward, cross her legs or use a low table, which will squash vital digestive organs, interrupt the flow of her blood and strain her spinal cord, the problem illustrated in a cautionary drawing.

She should instead be following the example of this maiden:

(ii) Corsets

Dr Proust did not hide his distaste for these fashion items, describing them as self-destructive and perverse [in an important distinction for anyone worried about the correlation between slimness and attractiveness, he informed readers that, 'The *thin* woman is far from being the *svelte* woman']. And in an attempt to warn off girls who might have been tempted to wear these corsets, Dr Proust included an illustration showing their catastrophic effect on the spinal cord.

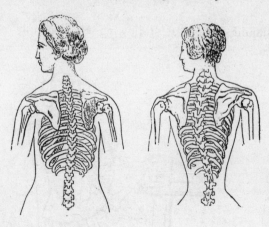

(iii) Exercise

Rather than pretending to be slim and fit through artificial means, Dr Proust proposed a regime of regular exercise and included a number of practical, unstrenuous examples – like, for instance, jumping off walls . . .

. . . hopping around . . .

. . . swinging one's arms . . .

. . . and balancing on one foot.

With a father so masterful at aerobic instruction, at advice on corsets and sewing positions, it seems as if Marcel may have been hasty or simply overambitious in equating his life's work with that of the author of *Elements of Hygiene*. Rather than blame him for the problem, one might ask whether *any* novel could genuinely be expected to contain therapeutic qualities, whether the genre could in itself offer any more relief than could be gained from an aspirin, a country walk or a dry martini.

Charitably, one could suggest escapism. Marooned in familiar circumstances, there may be pleasure in buying a paperback at the station news-stand ['I was attracted by the idea of reaching a wider audience, the sort of people who buy a badly printed volume before catching a train,' specified Proust]. Once we've boarded a carriage, we can abstract ourselves from current surroundings and enter a more agreeable, or at least agreeably different world, breaking off occasionally to take in the passing scenery, while holding open our badly printed volume at the point where an ill-tempered monocle-wearing baron prepares to enter his drawing room – until our destination is heard on the tannoy, the brakes let out their reluctant squeals and we emerge once more into reality, symbolized by the station and its group of loitering slate-grey pigeons pecking shiftily at abandoned confectionery [in her memoirs, Proust's maid Céleste helpfully informs those alarmed not to have made much ground in Proust's novel that it is not designed to be read from one station to the next].

Whatever the pleasures of using a novel as an object with which to levitate into another world, it is not the only way of handling the genre. It certainly wasn't Proust's way, and would arguably not have been a very effective method of fulfilling the exalted therapeutic ambitions expressed to Céleste.

Perhaps the best indication of Proust's views on how we should read lies in his approach to looking at paintings. After his death, his friend Lucien Daudet wrote an account of his time with him, which included a description of a visit they had once made together to the Louvre. Whenever he looked at paintings, Proust had a habit of trying to match the figures depicted on canvases with people he knew from his own life. Daudet tells us that they went into a gallery hung with a painting by Domenico Ghirlandaio. It was called *An Old Man and a Boy*, it had been painted in the 1480s and it showed a kindly looking man with a set of carbuncles on the tip of his nose.

Proust considered the Ghirlandaio for a moment, then turned to Daudet and told him that this man was the spitting image of the Marquis de Lau, a well-known figure in the Parisian social world.

How surprising to identify the Marquis, a gentleman in late-nineteenth-century Paris, in a portrait painted in Italy in the late fifteenth century. However, a snap of the Marquis survives. It shows him sitting in a garden with a group of ladies wearing the kind of elaborate dress you would need five maids to help you into. He has on a dark suit, a winged collar, cuff links and a top hat, but despite the nineteenth-century paraphernalia and the poor quality of the photo, one imagines that he might indeed have looked strikingly similar to the carbuncled man painted by Ghirlandaio in Renaissance Italy, a long-lost brother dramatically separated from him across countries and centuries.

The possibility of making such visual connections between people circulating in apparently wholly different worlds explains Proust's assertion that 'aesthetically, the number of human types is so restricted that we must constantly, wherever we may be, have the pleasure of seeing people we know'.

Any such pleasure is not simply visual: the restricted number of human types also means that we are repeatedly able to *read* about people we know in places we might never have expected to do so.

For instance, in the second volume of Proust's novel, the narrator visits the Normandy seaside resort of Balbec, where he meets and falls in love with someone I know, a young woman with an impudent expression, brilliant laughing eyes, plump matt cheeks and a fondness for black polo-caps. Here is Proust's portrait of what Albertine sounds like when she is talking.

> In speaking, Albertine kept her head motionless and her nostrils pinched, and scarcely moved her lips. The result of this was a drawling, nasal sound, into the composition of which there entered perhaps a provincial heredity, a juvenile affectation of British phlegm, the teaching of a foreign governess and a congestive hypertrophy of the mucus of the nose. This enunciation, which, as it happened, soon disappeared when she knew people better, giving place to a girlish tone, might have been thought unpleasant. But to me it was peculiarly delightful. Whenever I had gone for several days without seeing her,

I would refresh my spirit by repeating to myself: 'We don't ever see you playing golf,' with the nasal intonation in which she had uttered the words, point-blank, without moving a muscle of her face. And I thought then that there was no one in the world so desirable.

It is difficult when reading the description of certain fictional characters not at the same time to imagine the real-life acquaintances who they most closely, if often unexpectedly, resemble. It has, for example, proved impossible for me to separate Proust's Duchesse de Guermantes from the image of the fifty-five-year-old stepmother of an ex-girlfriend, even though this unsuspecting lady speaks no French, has no title and lives in Devon. What is more, when Proust's hesitant, shy character Saniette asks if he can visit the narrator in his hotel in Balbec, the proud, defensive tone with which he masks his friendly intentions seems exactly that of an old college acquaintance who had a manic habit of never putting himself in a situation where he might encounter rejection.

'You don't happen to know what you'll be doing in the next few days, because I will probably be somewhere in the neighbourhood of Balbec? Not that it makes the slightest difference, I just thought I'd ask,' says Saniette to the narrator, though it could equally well have been Philip proposing plans for an evening. As for Proust's Gilberte, she finds herself resolutely associated in my mind with Julia, who I met on a skiing holiday at the age of twelve, and who twice invited me for tea [she ate *millefeuilles* slowly, dropping crumbs on her print dress} and who I kissed on New Year's Eve and never saw again, for she lived in Africa, where she might today be a nurse if her adolescent wish came true.

How helpful of Proust to remark that, 'One cannot read a novel without ascribing to the heroine the traits of the one we love.' It lends respectability to a habit of imagining that Albertine, last seen walking in Balbec with her brilliant laughing eyes and black polo-cap, bears striking resemblance to my girlfriend Kate, who has never read Proust and prefers George Eliot, or *Marie Claire* after a difficult day.

Kate/Albertine

Such intimate communion between our own life and the novels we read may be why Proust argued that:

> In reality, every reader is, while he is reading, the reader of his own self. The writer's work is merely a kind of optical instrument which he offers to the reader to enable him to discern what, without this book, he would perhaps never have experienced in himself. And the recognition by the reader in his own self of what the book says is the proof of its veracity.

But why would readers seek to be the readers of their own selves? Why does Proust privilege the connection between ourselves and works of art, as much in his novel as in his museum habits?

One answer is because it is the only way in which art can properly affect rather than simply distract us from life, and that there is a stream of extraordinary benefits attached to what might be termed the *Marquis de Lau phenomenon* [MLP], attached to the possibility of recognizing Kate in a portrait of Albertine, Julia in a description of Gilberte and, more generally, our selves in badly printed volumes purchased in train stations.

Benefits of the MLP

(i) To feel at home everywhere
The fact we might be surprised to recognize someone we know in a portrait painted four centuries ago suggests how

hard it is to hold on to anything more than a theoretical belief in a universal human nature. As Proust saw the problem:

> People of bygone ages seem infinitely remote from us. We do not feel justified in ascribing to them any underlying intentions beyond those they formally express; we are amazed when we come across an emotion more or less like what we feel today in a Homeric hero ... it is as though we imagined the epic poet ... to be as remote from ourselves as an animal seen in a zoo.

It is perhaps only normal if our initial impulse on being introduced to the characters of *The Odyssey* is to stare at them as though they are a family of duck-billed platypuses circling their enclosure in the municipal zoo. Bewilderment might be no less intense at the thought of listening to a louche character with a thick moustache, standing in the midst of distinctly antiquated-looking friends:

But an advantage of more prolonged encounters with Proust or Homer is that worlds that had seemed threateningly alien reveal themselves to be essentially much like our own, expanding the range of places in which we feel at home. It means we can open the zoo gates and release a set of trapped creatures from the Trojan War or the Faubourg Saint-Germain, who we had previously considered with unwarranted provincial suspicion, because they had names like Eurycleia and Telemachus or had never sent a fax.

(ii) A cure for loneliness
We might also let *ourselves* out from the zoo. What is considered normal for a person to feel in any place at any point is liable to be an abbreviated version of what is in fact normal, so that the experiences of fictional characters afford us a hugely expanded picture of human behaviour, and thereby a confirmation of the essential normality of thoughts or feelings unmentioned in our immediate environment. After childishly picking a fight with a lover who had looked distracted throughout dinner, there is relief in hearing Proust's narrator admit to us that 'As soon as I found Albertine not being nice to me, instead of telling her I was sad, I became nasty', and revealing that 'I never expressed a desire to break up with her except when I was unable to do without her', after which our own romantic antics might seem less like those of a perverse platypus.

MLPs can similarly make us feel less lonely. After being abandoned by a lover who has expressed in the kindest way imaginable a need to spend a little more time on their own, how consoling to lie in bed and witness Proust's narrator crystallizing the thought that, 'When two people part it is the one who is not in love who makes the tender speeches.' How comforting to witness a fictional person [who is also, miraculously, ourselves as we read] suffering the same agonies of a saccharine dismissal and, importantly, surviving.

(iii) The finger placing ability

The value of a novel is not limited to its depiction of emotions and people akin to those in our own life, it stretches to an ability to describe these *far better* than we would have been able, to put a finger on perceptions that we recognize *as our own*, yet could not have formulated *on our own*.

We might have known someone like the fictional Duchesse de Guermantes, and felt there was something superior and insolent in her manner, without knowing quite what, until Proust discreetly pointed out in brackets how the Duchesse reacted when, during a smart dinner, a Mme de Gallardon made the error of being a little overfamiliar with the Duchesse, known also as Oriane des Laumes, and addressed her by her first name:

'Oriane,' (at once Mme des Laumes looked with amused

astonishment towards an invisible third person, whom she seemed to call to witness that she had never authorized Mme de Gallardon to use her Christian name) . . .

An effect of reading a book which has devoted attention to noticing such faint yet vital tremors is that, once we've put the volume down and resumed our own life, we may attend to precisely the things which the author would have responded to had he or she been in our company. Our mind will be like a radar newly attuned to pick up certain objects floating through consciousness, the effect will be like bringing a radio into a room that we had thought silent, and realizing that the silence only existed at a particular frequency and that all along we in fact shared the room with waves of sound coming in from a Ukrainian station or the night-time chatter of a minicab firm. Our attention will be drawn to the shades of the sky, to the changeability of a face, to the hypocrisy of a friend or to a submerged sadness about a situation which we had previously not even known we could feel sad about. The book will have *sensitized* us, stimulated our dormant antennae by evidence of its own developed sensitivity.

Which is why Proust proposed, in words he would modestly never have extended to his own novel, that:

If we read the new masterpiece of a man of genius, we are delighted to find in it those reflections of ours that we despised, joys and sorrows which we had repressed, a whole world of feeling we had scorned and whose value the book in which we discover them suddenly teaches us.

CHAPTER THREE

How to Take
Your Time

Whatever the merits of Proust's work, even a fervent admirer would be hard pressed to deny one of its awkward features: length. As Proust's brother, Robert, put it, 'The sad thing is that people have to be very ill or have broken a leg in order to have the opportunity to read *In Search of Lost Time*.' And as they lie in bed with their limb newly encased in plaster or a tubercular bacillus diagnosed in their lungs, they face another challenge in the length of individual Proustian sentences, snake-like constructions, the very longest of which, located in the fifth volume, would, if arranged along a single line in standard-sized text, run on for a little short of four metres and stretch around the base of a bottle of wine seventeen times:

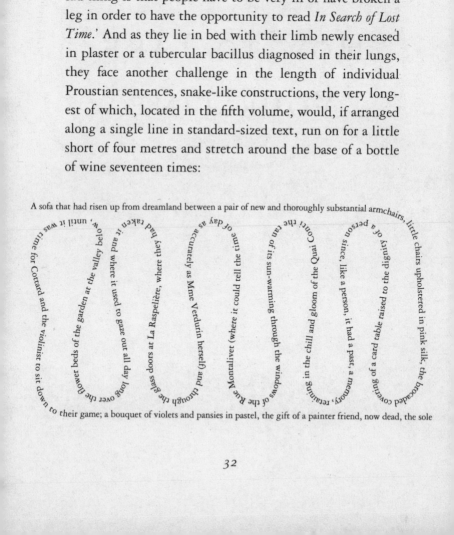

A sofa that had risen up from dreamland between a pair of new and thoroughly substantial armchairs, little chairs upholstered in pink silk, the brocaded covering of a card table raised to the dignity of a person since, like a person, it had a past, a memory, retaining in the chill and gloom of the Quai Conti the ran of its sun-warming through the windows of the Rue Montalivet (where it could tell the time of day as accurately as Mme Verdurin herself) and through the glass doors at La Raspelière, where they had taken it and where it used to gaze out all day long over the flower beds of the garden at the valley below', until it was time for Cotard and the violinist to sit down to their game; a bouquet of violets and pansies in pastel, the gift of a painter friend, now dead, the sole

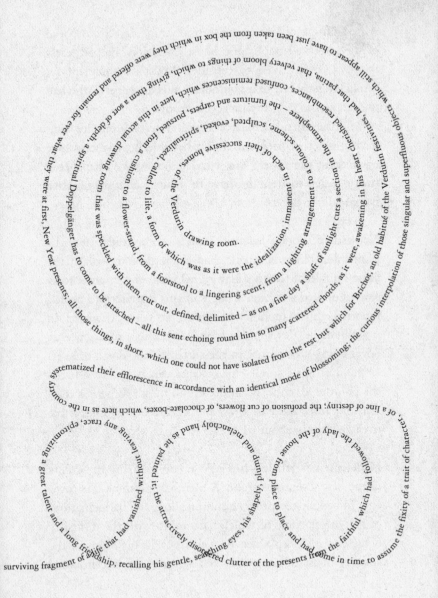

the furniture and carpets, pursued, evoked, spiritualized, here in this actual drawing room, giving them a sort of depth, a spiritual Doppelgänger has to come to be attached — all this sent echoing round him so many scattered chords, as it were, awakening in his heart cherished resemblances, confused reminiscences which, here in this actual drawing room that was speckled with them, cut out, defined, delimited — as on a fine day a shaft of sunlight cuts a section in the atmosphere — the velvety bloom of things to which they were offered and remain for ever what they were at first, New Year presents; all those things, in short, which one could not have isolated from the rest but which for Brichot, an old habitué of the Verdurin festivities, had that patina, that velvety bloom of things to which, from a colour scheme to a flower-stand, to a cushion, a form of which was as it were the idealization, immanent in each of their successive homes, from a footstool to a lingering scent, sculpted, evoked, spiritualized, from a lighting arrangement, of the Verdurin drawing room.

systematized their efflorescence in accordance with an identical mode of blossoming; the curious interpolation of those singular and superfluous objects which still appear to have just been taken from the box in which they were

of a line of destiny; the profusion of cut flowers, of chocolate-boxes, which here as in the country

a great talent and a long friend- life that had vanished without leaving any trace, epitomizing

the attractively disordering eyes, his shapely, plump and melancholy hand as he painted it; the

followed the lady of the house from place to place and had on the faithful which had come in time to assume the fixity of a trait of character, of a character

surviving fragment of a friendship, recalling his gentle, scattered clutter of the presents from... come in time to assume

Alfred Humblot had never seen anything like it. As head of the esteemed publishing house Ollendorf, he had, early in 1913, been asked to consider Proust's manuscript for publication by one of his authors, Louis de Robert, who had undertaken to help Proust get into print.

'My dear friend, I may be dense,' replied Humblot after having taken a brief and clearly bewildering glance at the opening of the novel, 'but I fail to see why a chap needs thirty pages to describe how he tosses and turns in bed before falling asleep.'

He wasn't alone. Jacques Madeleine, a reader for the publishing house Fasquelle, had been asked to look at the same bundle of papers a few months earlier. 'At the end of seven hundred and twelve pages of this manuscript,' he had reported, 'after innumerable griefs at being drowned in unfathomable developments and irritating impatience at never being able to rise to the surface – one doesn't have a single, but not a single clue of what this is about. What is the point of all this? What does it all mean? Where is it all leading? Impossible to know anything about it! Impossible to say anything about it!'

Madeleine nevertheless had a go at summarizing the events of the first seventeen pages: 'A man has insomnia. He turns over in bed, he recaptures his impressions and hallucinations of half-sleep, some of which have to do with the difficulty of getting to sleep when he was a boy in his room in the country house of his parents in Combray. Seventeen pages!

Where one sentence (at the end of page 4 and page 5) goes on for forty-four lines.'

As all other publishers sympathized with these sentiments, Proust was forced to pay for the publication of his work himself [and was left to enjoy the regrets and contrite apologies which flowed in a few years later]. But the accusation of verbosity was not so fleeting. At the end of 1921, his work now widely acclaimed, Proust received a letter from an American, who described herself as twenty-seven, resident in Rome and extremely beautiful. She also explained that for the previous three years she had done nothing with her time other than read Proust's book. However, there was a problem: 'I don't understand a thing, but absolutely nothing. Dear Marcel Proust, stop being a poseur and come down to earth. Just tell me in two lines what you really wanted to say.'

The frustration of the Roman beauty suggests that the poseur had violated a fundamental law of length stipulating the appropriate number of words in which an experience could be related. He had not written too much *per se*; he had digressed intolerably given the significance of the events under consideration. Falling asleep? Two words should cover it, four lines if the hero had indigestion or an Alsatian was giving birth in the courtyard below. But the poseur hadn't digressed simply about sleep, he had made the same error with dinner parties, seductions, jealousies.

It explains the inspiration behind the 'All-England Summarize Proust Competition', once hosted by Monty Python in a south coast seaside resort, a competition which required contestants to précis the seven volumes of Proust's work in fifteen seconds or less, and to deliver the results in a swimsuit and evening dress. The initial contestant was Harry Baggot from Luton, who hurriedly offered the following:

> *'Proust's novel ostensibly tells of the irrevocability of time lost, of innocence and experience, the reinstatement of extratemporal values and time regained. Ultimately the novel is both optimistic and set within the context of human religious experience. In the first volume, Swann visits—'*

But fifteen seconds did not allow for more. 'A good attempt,' declared the game-show host with dubious sincerity, 'but unfortunately he chose a general appraisal of the work before getting on to specific details.' The contestant was thanked for his attempt, commended on his swimming trunks and shown off stage.

Despite this personal defeat, the contest as a whole remained optimistic that an acceptable summary of Proust's work was possible, a faith that what had originally taken seven volumes to express could reasonably be condensed into fifteen seconds or less, without too great a loss of integrity or meaning, if only an appropriate candidate could be found.

What did Proust have for breakfast? Before his illness became too severe, two cups of strong coffee with milk, served in a silver pot engraved with his initials. He liked his coffee tightly packed in a filter with the water made to pass through drop by drop. He also had a croissant, fetched by his maid from a boulangerie which knew just how to make them, crisp and buttery, and which he would dunk in his coffee as he looked through his letters and read the newspaper.

He had complex feelings about the last activity. However unusual the attempt to compress seven volumes of a novel into fifteen seconds, perhaps nothing exceeds, in both regularity and scope, the compression entailed by a daily newspaper. Stories which would comfortably fill twenty volumes find themselves reduced to narrow columns, competing for the reader's attention with a multitude of once profound, now etiolated dramas.

'That abominable and sensual act called *reading the newspaper*,' wrote Proust, 'thanks to which all the misfortunes and cataclysms in the universe over the last twenty-four hours, the battles which cost the lives of fifty thousand men, the murders, the strikes, the bankruptcies, the fires, the poisonings, the suicides, the divorces, the cruel emotions of statesmen and actors, are transformed for us, who don't even care, into a morning treat, blending in wonderfully, in a particularly exciting and tonic way, with the recommended ingestion of a few sips of *café au lait*.'

Of course, it shouldn't surprise us how naturally the thought of another sip of coffee could derail our attempt to consider with requisite care those closely packed, perhaps now crumb-littered pages. The more an account is compressed, the more it seems that it deserves no more space than it has been allocated. How easy to imagine that nothing at all has happened today, to forget the fifty thousand war dead, sigh, toss the paper to one side and experience a mild wave of melancholy at the tedium of daily routine.

It was not Proust's way. An entire philosophy, not only of reading but of life, could be said to emerge from Lucien Daudet's passing remark, informing us that:

> He read newspapers with great care. He wouldn't even overlook the news-in-brief section. A news-in-brief told by him turned into a whole tragic or comic novel, thanks to his imagination and his fantasy.

The news-in-brief in *Le Figaro*, Proust's daily paper, was not for the faint-hearted. On a particular morning in May 1914, readers would have been graced with some of the following:

> At a busy crossing in Villeurbanne, a horse leapt into the rear carriage of a tram, overturning all the passengers, of whom three were seriously injured and had to be taken to hospital.

> While introducing a friend to the workings of an

electric power station in Aube, M. Marcel Peigny put a finger on a high-voltage cable and was at once fatally electrocuted.

A teacher, M. Jules Renard, committed suicide yesterday in the Métropolitain, in the République station, by firing a single revolver shot into his chest. M. Renard had been suffering from an incurable disease.

What sort of tragic or comic novels would these have swelled into? Jules Renard? An unhappily married, asthmatic chemistry teacher employed by a Left Bank girls' school, diagnosed with colon cancer, echoes of Balzac, Dostoevsky and Zola. The electrocuted Marcel Peigny? Killed while impressing a friend with a knowledge of electrical hardware in order to encourage a union between his harelipped son, Serge, and his friend's uncorseted daughter, Mathilde. And the horse in Villeurbanne? A somersault into the tram provoked by misjudged nostalgia for a show-jumping career, or vengeance for the omnibus which had recently killed its brother in the market square, later put down for horse steak, suitable for feuilleton format.

A more sober example of Proust's inflationary efforts survives. In January 1907, he was reading the paper when his eye was caught by a headline of a news-in-brief, which read, *A Tragedy of Madness*. A bourgeois young man, Henri van Blarenberghe, had, 'in a fit of madness', stabbed and killed his mother with a kitchen knife. She had cried out,

'Henri, Henri, what have you done to me?' raised her arms to the sky and collapsed on the floor. Henri had then locked himself in his room and tried to cut his throat with the knife, but he had had difficulties severing the right vein, and so had put a revolver to his temple. Yet he wasn't an expert with this weapon either, and when the police officers [one of whom happened to be called Proust] arrived at the scene they found him in his room, lying on his bed, his face a mess, one eye dangling by connecting tissue out of a blood-filled socket. They began to interrogate him about the incident with his mother outside, but he died before an adequate statement could be drawn up.

Proust might quickly have turned the page and taken an extra gulp of coffee had he not happened to be an acquaintance of the murderer. He had met the polite and sensitive Henri van Blarenberghe at a number of dinner parties, they had exchanged a few letters thereafter, indeed Proust had received one only a few weeks earlier, in which the young man had enquired into his health, wondered what the new year would bring for them both, and hoped he and Proust would be able to meet up again soon.

Alfred Humblot, Jacques Madeleine and the beautiful American correspondent from Rome would possibly have judged that the correct literary response to this grim crime was an appalled word or two. Proust wrote a five-page article instead, in which he attempted to place the squalid tale of dangling eyeballs and kitchen utensils back into a broader context, judging it not as a freak murder defying precedent or understanding, but rather as a manifestation of a tragic aspect of human nature which had been at the centre of many of the greatest works of Western art since the Greeks. For Proust, Henri's blindness while he stabbed his mother linked him to the confused fury of Ajax massacring the Greek shepherds and their flocks. Henri was Oedipus, his dangling eye an echo of the way Oedipus had used the gold buckles from the dead Jocasta's dress to puncture his own eyeballs. The devastation Henri must have felt at seeing his dead mother reminded Proust of Lear embracing the body of Cordelia, and crying out: 'She's gone for ever. She's dead as earth. No, no, no life! Why should a dog, a horse, a rat, have life, And thou no breath at all?' And when police officer Proust had arrived to question Henri as he lay expiring, the author Proust had felt like acting as Kent had done when telling Edgar not to awake the unconscious Lear: 'Vex not his ghost: Oh! let him pass; he hates him that would upon the rack of this tough world stretch him out longer.'

These literary quotations were not simply designed to impress [though Proust did happen to feel that 'One must never miss an opportunity of quoting things by others which are always more interesting than those one thinks up oneself']. Rather they were a way of alluding to the universal implications of matricide. For Proust, van Blarenberghe's crime had something to say to everyone, we could not judge it as though wholly unrelated to its dynamics. Even if we had only forgotten to send Mother a birthday card, we would have to recognize a trace of our guilt in the death cries of Mme van Blarenberghe. '"*What have you done to me! What have you done to me!*" If we wanted to think about it,' wrote Proust, 'perhaps there is no really loving mother who could not, on her dying day, and often long before, address this reproach to her son. The truth is that as we grow older we kill all those who love us by the cares we give them, by the anxious tenderness we inspire in them and constantly arouse.'

By such efforts, a story that had seemed to deserve no more than a gruesome few lines in a news-in-brief had been integrated into the history of tragedy and mother–son relationships, its dynamics observed with the complex sympathy one would usually accord to Oedipus on stage, but consider inappropriate, even shocking, when lavished on a murderer from the morning paper.

It shows how vulnerable much of human experience is to abbreviation, how easily it can be stripped of the more obvious signposts by which we guide ourselves when ascribing importance. Much literature and drama would conceivably have proved entirely unengaging, would have said nothing to us had we first encountered its subject matter over breakfast in the form of news-in-brief.

> Tragic end for Verona lovebirds: after mistakenly
> thinking his sweetheart dead, a young man took his

life. Having discovered the fate of her lover, the
woman killed herself in turn.

A young mother threw herself under a train and
died in Russia after domestic problems.

A young mother took arsenic and died in a French
provincial town after domestic problems.

Unfortunately, the very artistry of Shakespeare, Tolstoy and
Flaubert has the tendency to suggest that it would have
been apparent even from a news-in-brief that there was
something significant about Romeo, Anna and Emma,
something which would have led any right-thinking person
to see that these were characters fit for great literature or a
show at the Globe, whereas of course there would have been
nothing to distinguish them from the somersaulting horse
in Villeurbanne or the electrocuted Marcel Peigny in Aube.
Hence Proust's assertion that the greatness of works of art
has nothing to do with the apparent quality of their subject
matter, and everything to do with the subsequent treatment
of that matter. And hence his associated claims that
everything is potentially a fertile subject for art and that we
can make discoveries as valuable in an advertisement for
soap as in Pascal's *Pensées*.

Blaise Pascal was born in 1623, and was recognized from
an early age – and by more than just his proud family – to
be a genius. By twelve he had worked out the first thirty-
two propositions of Euclid; he went on to invent the

mathematics of probability, he measured atmospheric pressure, constructed a calculating machine, designed an omnibus, got tuberculosis and wrote the brilliant and pessimistic series of aphorisms in defence of Christian belief known as the *Pensées*.

It would be no surprise to discover things of value in the *Pensées*. The work occupies a privileged cultural position, which encourages us to take our time over it and imagine that we, rather than the author, would be to blame if we ended up unable to see the point. Not that this is likely to happen, for the *Pensées* are written with seductive immediacy, broaching topics of universal concern with modern succinctness. 'We do not choose as captain of a ship the most highly born of those aboard,' runs one aphorism, and we can admire the dry irony of this protest against inherited privilege, which must have been so galling in the unmeritocratic society of Pascal's day. The habit of putting people into important offices simply because they had important parents is quietly ridiculed by an analogy between statecraft and navigation: Pascal's readers might have been intimidated and silenced by an aristocrat's elaborate argument that he had a divine right to determine economic policy, even though he had failed to master the upper reaches of the seven times table, but they would be unlikely to swallow a similar argument from a duke if he knew nothing of sailing and was proposing to take the wheel on a journey around the Cape of Good Hope.

How frothy the soap looks besides this. How far we have
drifted from the spiritual realm with this long-haired
maiden, clutching her bosom in rapture at the thought of
her toilet soap, handily kept with the necklaces in a padded
jewellery box.

PEARS'

The "Jewel" of all Toilet Soaps

It seems difficult to argue that soapy bliss is truly as
significant as Pascal's *Pensées*. But it was not Proust's
intention, he was merely saying that a soap advertisement
could be the starting point for thoughts which might end
up being no less profound than those already well expressed,
already well developed in the *Pensées*. If we were unlikely to
have had deep thoughts with toilet soaps before, it could

merely have been out of adherence to conventional notions of where to have such thoughts, a resistance to the spirit which had guided Flaubert in turning a newspaper story about the suicide of a young wife into *Madame Bovary*, or the spirit which had guided Proust in taking on the initially unprepossessing topic of falling asleep and devoting thirty pages to it.

A similar spirit appears to have guided Proust in his reading matter. His friend Maurice Duplay tells us that what Marcel most liked reading when he couldn't get to sleep was a train timetable.

Numéro de train		88101	88045	88047	3131	13161	3133	3139
Notes à consulter		1	2	1	2	3	1	2
Paris-St-Lazare	D				06.42	07.39	07.55	**09.15**
Mantes la Jolie	D					08.11		
Vernon (Eure)	D				07.23	08.24		
Gaillon-Aubevoye	D					08.34		
Val-de-Reuil	D					08.46		
Oissel	D	05.56				08.56		
Rouen-Rive-Droite	A	06.12			07.56	09.08	09.04	**10.26**
Rouen-Rive-Droite	D		06.20	06.50	08.00	09.10	09.06	**10.28**
Yvetot	A		06.48	07.26	08.20	09.34	09.26	**10.48**
Bréauté-Beuzeville	A		07.08	07.46	08.35	09.48		11.02
Le Havre	A		07.24	08.15	08.51	10.04	09.51	**11.18**

1. Circule: tous les jours sauf les dim et fêtes.

2. Circule: tous les jours sauf les dim et fêtes – .

3. Circule: les dim et fêtes.

The departure time of the St-Lazare train was not the point for a man who found no reason to leave Paris in the last eight years of his life. Rather, the timetable was read and enjoyed as though it were a gripping novel about country life, because the mere names of provincial train stations provided Proust's imagination with material to elaborate entire worlds, to picture domestic dramas in rural villages, shenanigans in local government and life out in the fields.

Proust argued that enjoyment of such wayward reading matter was typical of a writer, someone who could be counted upon to develop enthusiasms for things that were apparently out of line with great art, a person for whom:

> a terrible musical production in a provincial theatre, or a ball which people of taste find ridiculous, will either evoke memories or else be linked to an order of reveries and preoccupations, far more than some admirable performance at the Opéra or an ultra-smart soirée in the Faubourg Saint-Germain. The names of northern railway stations in a timetable, where he would like to imagine himself stepping from the train on an autumn evening, when the trees are already bare and smelling strongly in the keen air, an insipid publication for people of taste, full of names he has not heard since childhood, may have far greater value for him than fine volumes of philosophy, and lead people of taste to say that for a man of talent, he has very stupid tastes.

Or at least, unconventional tastes. This often became apparent to people who met Proust for the first time, and were quizzed on aspects of their life which they had previously considered with all the meagre spiritual attention usually paid to adverts for household goods and timetables from Paris to Le Havre.

In 1919, the young diplomat Harold Nicolson was introduced to Proust at a party at the Ritz. Nicolson had been posted to Paris with the British delegation at the peace conference following the Great War, an assignment he found interesting, but clearly not as interesting as Proust turned out to find it.

In his diary, Nicolson reported of the party:

> A swell affair. Proust is white, unshaven, grubby, slip-faced. He asks me questions. Will I please tell him how the Committees work. I say, 'Well, we generally meet at 10.00, there are secretaries behind . . .' *'Mais non, mais non, vous allez trop vite. Recommencez. Vous prenez la voiture de la Délégation. Vous descendez au Quai d'Orsay. Vous montez l'escalier. Vous entrez dans la Salle. Et alors? Précisez, mon cher, précisez.'* So I tell him everything. The sham cordiality of it all: the handshakes: the maps: the rustle of papers: the tea in the next room: the macaroons. He listens enthralled, interrupting from time to time − *'Mais précisez, mon cher monsieur, n'allez pas trop vite.'*

It might be a Proustian slogan: *n'allez pas trop vite*. And an advantage of not going by too fast is that the world has a chance of becoming more interesting in the process. For Nicolson, an early morning that had been summed up by the terse statement, 'Well, we generally meet at ten,' had been expanded to reveal handshakes and maps, rustling papers and macaroons – the macaroon acting as a useful symbol, in its seductive sweetness, of what gets noticed when we don't go by *trop vite*.

Less greedily, more importantly, going by slowly may entail greater sympathy. We are being a good deal more sympathetic to the disturbed Mr van Blarenberghe in writing an extended meditation on his crime than in muttering *crazy* and turning the page.

And expansion brings similar benefits to non-criminal activity. Proust's narrator spends an unusual number of pages of the novel describing a painful indecision; he doesn't know whether to propose marriage to his girlfriend Albertine, who he sometimes thinks he couldn't live without, and at other times is certain he never wants to see again.

The problem could be résuméd in under two seconds by a skilled contestant from the All-England Summarize Proust competition: *Young man unsure whether or not to propose marriage*. Though not as brief as this, the letter which the narrator one day receives from his mother expresses his marriage dilemma in terms which make his previous, copious analysis look shamefully exaggerated. After reading it, the narrator tells himself:

I've been dreaming, the matter is quite simple . . . I am an indecisive young man, and it is a case of one of those marriages where it takes time to find out whether it will happen or not. There is nothing in this peculiar to Albertine.

Simple accounts are not without their pleasures. Suddenly, we are just 'insecure', 'homesick', 'settling in', 'facing up to death' or 'afraid of letting go'. It can be soothing to identify with a description of a problem which makes a previous assessment look needlessly complicated.

But it usually isn't. A moment after reading the letter, the narrator reconsiders and realizes that there must be more to his story with Albertine than his mother has suggested, and so he once again sides with length, with the hundreds of pages he has devoted to charting every shift in his relation with Albertine [*n'allez pas trop vite*], and comments:

> One can of course reduce everything, if one regards it in its social aspect, to the most commonplace item of newspaper gossip. From outside, it is perhaps thus that I myself would look at it. But I know very well that what is true, what at least is also true, is everything that I have thought, what I have read in Albertine's eyes, the fears that torment me, the problem that I continually put to myself with regard to Albertine. The story of the hesitant suitor and the broken engagement may correspond to this, as the report of a theatrical performance made by an intelligent reporter may give us the subject

of one of Ibsen's plays. But there is something beyond those facts that are reported.

The lesson? To hang on to the performance, to read the newspaper as though it were only the tip of a tragic or comic novel and to use thirty pages to describe a fall into sleep when need be. And if there is no time, at least to resist the approach of Alfred Humblot at Ollendorf and Jacques Madeleine at Fasquelle, which Proust defined as, 'the self-satisfaction felt by "busy" men – however idiotic their business – at "not having time" to do what you are doing'.

CHAPTER FOUR

How to Suffer Successfully

A good way of evaluating the wisdom of someone's ideas might be to undertake a careful examination of the state of their own mind and health. After all, if their pronouncements were truly worthy of our attention, we should expect that the first person to reap their benefits would be their creator. Might this justify an interest not simply in a writer's work, but also in their life?

Sainte-Beuve, the respected nineteenth-century critic, would have eagerly concurred:

> Until such time as one has put to oneself a certain number of questions about an author, and has answered them, be it only to oneself alone and under one's breath, one cannot be sure of having grasped him completely, even though the questions may seem quite foreign to the nature of his writings: What were his religious ideas? How did the spectacle of nature affect him? How did he behave in the matter of women, of money? Was he rich, poor; what was his diet, his daily routine? What was his vice or his weakness? None of the answers to these questions is irrelevant.

Even so, the answers tend to be surprising. However brilliant, however wise the work, it seems that the lives of artists can be relied upon to exhibit an extraordinary, incongruous range of turmoil, misery and stupidity.

It accounts for why Proust dismissed Sainte-Beuve's thesis, and argued forcefully that it was the books, not the lives, that mattered. That way, one could be sure of appreciating what was important ['It's true that there are people who are superior to their books, but that's because their books are not *Books*']. Balzac may have been ill-mannered, Stendhal conversationally dull and Baudelaire obsessive, but why should this colour our approach to their works which suffer from none of the faults of their creators?

Whatever the persuasiveness of the argument, it is easy to see why Proust should have been especially keen on it. Whereas his writing was logical, well constructed, often serene, even sagelike, he led a life of appalling physical and psychological suffering. While it is clear why someone might be interested in developing a Proustian approach to life, the sane would never harbour a desire to lead a life like Proust's.

Could this degree of suffering really be allowed to pass by without raising suspicion? Could Proust really have known much, could he have had anything valid to say to us, *and* still have led such a difficult, unexemplary life? Can the proof be allowed to stand so far from Sainte-Beuve's pudding?

The life certainly was a trial. The psychological problems were exhaustive enough.

— The Problem of a Jewish Mother

Proust was born into the clutches of a recklessly extreme example. 'I was always four years old for her,' said Marcel of Mme Proust, otherwise known as Maman, or more usually '*chère petite Maman*'.

'He never said "*ma mère*" nor "*mon père*", but always only "*Papa*" and "*Maman*" in the tone of an emotional little boy, with tears automatically welling up in his eyes as soon as these syllables had been uttered, while the hoarse sound of a strangled sob could be heard in his tightened throat,' recalled Proust's friend Marcel Plantevignes.

Mme Proust loved her son with an intensity that would have put an ardent lover to shame, an affection that created, or at the very least dramatically aggravated, her eldest son's disposition towards helplessness. There was nothing she felt he could do properly without her. They lived together from his birth until her death, by which time he was thirty-four. Even so, her greatest anxiety was whether Marcel would be able to survive in the world once she had gone. 'My mother wanted to live in order not to leave me in the state of anguish which she knew I was in without her,' he explained after her death, 'all of our life had been simply a training, she for teaching me how to do without her the day she would leave me ... And I, for my part, I persuaded her that I could quite well live without her.'

Though well-meaning, Mme Proust's concern for her son was never far from bossy intervention. At the age of twenty-four, in a rare moment when they were apart, Marcel wrote to tell her that he was sleeping quite well [the quality of his sleep, his stool and his appetite was a constant concern in their correspondence]. But Maman complained that he was not being precise enough: 'My darling, your "slept so many hours" continues to tell me nothing or rather nothing that counts. I ask and ask again:

You went to sleep at . . .

You got up at . . .'

Marcel was usually happy to fulfil his mother's controlling desire for corporeal information [she and Sainte-Beuve would have had much to talk about]. From time to time, Marcel spontaneously offered something up for general family consideration: 'Ask Papa what it means to feel a burning sensation at the moment of peeing which forces you to interrupt, then to restart, five or six times in quarter of an hour. As I've been drinking oceans of beer these days, perhaps it comes from that,' he mused in a letter to his mother; at which point, Maman was fifty-three, Papa was sixty-eight and Marcel thirty-one.

In answer to a questionnaire asking Proust for *Your notion of unhappiness*, he replied, 'To be separated from Maman.' When he couldn't sleep at night and his mother was in her bedroom, he would write letters which he would leave at her door for her to find in the morning. 'My dear little Maman,' ran a typical example, 'I am writing you a note while I'm finding it impossible to sleep, to tell you that I am thinking of you.'

Despite such correspondence, there were predictably underlying tensions. Marcel sensed that his mother preferred him to be ill and dependent rather than healthy and peeing well: 'The truth is that as soon as I am better, because the life which makes me get better annoys you, you ruin everything until I am ill again,' he wrote in a rare, though significant, outburst against Mme Proust's crippling desire to enact a nurse–patient relationship with him. 'It is sad not to be able to have at the same time affection and health.'

— *Awkward Desires*

Then came the slow recognition that Marcel was not like other boys. 'No one can tell at first whether he is an invert, or a poet, or a snob or a scoundrel. The boy who has been reading erotic poetry or looking at obscene pictures, if he then presses his body against a schoolfriend, only imagines himself to be communing with him in an identical desire for a woman. How should he suppose that he is not like everybody else when he recognizes the substance of what he feels in reading Mme de La Fayette, Racine, Baudelaire, Walter Scott?'

Yet gradually Proust realized that the prospect of a night with Scott's Diana Vernon held none of the attractions of being pressed up against a schoolfriend, a difficult realization given the unenlightened state of the France of his day, and a mother who continued to hope that her son would marry and displayed a habit of asking his male friends to bring along young women when they took Marcel out to the theatre or a restaurant.

— *Dating Problems*

If only she had poured her energies into inviting the other gender, for it wasn't easy to find young men similarly disenchanted with Diana Vernon. 'You think me jaded and effete. You are mistaken,' Proust protested to one recalcitrant candidate, a pretty sixteen-year-old classmate called Daniel Halévy. 'If you are delicious, if you have lovely eyes . . . , if your body and mind . . . are so lithe and tender that I feel I could mingle more intimately with your thoughts by sitting on your lap . . . , there is nothing in all that to deserve your contemptuous words.'

Rebuffs led Proust to justify his desire with selective appeals to the history of Western philosophy. 'I am glad to say that I have some highly intelligent friends, distinguished by great moral delicacy, who have amused themselves at one time with a boy,' Proust informed Daniel. 'That was the beginning of their youth. Later on they went back to women . . . I would like to speak to you of two masters of consummate wisdom, who in all their lives plucked only the bloom, Socrates and Montaigne. They permit men in their earliest youth to "amuse themselves", so as to know something of all pleasures, and so as to release their excess tenderness. They held that these at once sensual and intellectual friendships are better for a young man with a keen sense of beauty and awakened "senses", than affairs with stupid, corrupt women.'

Nevertheless, the blinkered boy continued in his pursuit of the stupid and the corrupt.

— *Romantic Pessimism*

'Love is an incurable disease.' 'In love, there is permanent suffering.' 'Those who love and those who are happy are not the same.'

Even the staunchest opponent of Sainte-Beuve might suspect that art had in this area been affected by a grief in the author's life. Proust's romantic pessimism was at least partly founded on the combination of an intense need for love and a tragicomic clumsiness in securing it. 'My only consolation when I am really sad is to love and to be loved,' he declared, and defined his principal character trait as 'the need to be loved; more precisely, a need to be petted and spoilt more than a need to be admired'. But an adolescence filled with misguided seductions of school-friends led to an equally fruitless adulthood. There were a succession of crushes on young men who didn't call back. In the seaside resort of Cabourg in 1911, Proust expressed his frustration to the young Albert Nahmias: 'If only I could change sex and age, take on the looks of a young and pretty woman in order to embrace you with all my heart.' For a time, there was a modicum of happiness with Alfred Agostinelli, a taxi driver who moved into Proust's flat with his wife, but Alfred met a premature end in a plane crash off Antibes, and thereafter there were to be no profound emotional engagements, merely further pronouncements on the inseparability of love and suffering.

— *A Lack of a Career in the Theatre*
Despite the pitfalls of psychobiographical speculation, it seems that there were underlying emotional difficulties focused on the integration of amorous and sexual emotions, a claim best illustrated by quoting a proposal for a play

which Proust sent to Reynaldo Hahn in 1906. It was to run as follows:

> A couple adore each other, immense affection, saintly, pure (needless to say, chaste) of the husband for his wife. But this man is a sadist and, besides the love for his wife, he has relations with whores, where he finds pleasure in soiling his own feelings. Finally, the sadist, always needing something stronger, comes to soil his wife in talking to these whores, in asking them to say bad things about her, and to say them himself (he is sickened five minutes after). While he is talking like this once, his wife comes into the room without him hearing. She can't believe her eyes or ears, falls. Then she leaves her husband. He begs, to no avail. The whores want to come back, but sadism would be too painful for him now, and after a last attempt to reconquer his wife, who doesn't even answer him, he kills himself.

Sadly, no Paris theatre manifested an interest.

— *The Incomprehension of Friends*
A characteristic problem for geniuses. When *Swann's Way* was ready Proust sent copies to his friends, many of whom had difficulty opening the envelope.

'Well, my dear Louis, have you read my book?' Proust recalled asking the aristocratic playboy, Louis d'Albufera.

'Read your book? You've written a book?' answered his surprised friend.

'Yes, of course, Louis, and I even sent you a copy.'

'Ah, my little Marcel, if you sent it to me, I've certainly read it. Only I wasn't sure I'd received it.'

Madame Gaston de Caillavet was a more grateful recipient. She wrote to thank the author for his gift in the warmest terms. 'I constantly reread the passage in *Swann* about first Communion,' she told him, 'as I experienced the same panic, the same disillusionment.' It was a touching thought for Madame Gaston de Caillavet to share – it might have been kinder had she taken the trouble to read the book and noticed that there was no such religious ceremony within it.

Proust concluded, 'About a book published only a few months earlier, people never speak to me without mistakes proving either that they've forgotten it or that they haven't read it.'

— *At Thirty, His Own Assessment*
'Without pleasures, objectives, activities or ambitions, with the life ahead of me finished and with an awareness of the grief I cause my parents, I have little happiness.'

As for a list of Proust's physical afflictions:

— *Asthma*
Attacks start when he is ten, and continue all his life. They are particularly severe, the fits lasting over an hour, as many as ten a day. Because they occur more in the daytime than at night, Proust takes up a nocturnal routine; he goes to sleep at seven in the morning and wakes up at four or five

in the afternoon. He finds it impossible to go much outdoors, particularly in the summer, and when he has to, it is only in the confines of a sealed taxi. The windows and curtains of his flat are kept perennially shut, he never sees the sun, breathes any fresh air, nor takes any exercise.

— Diet

He gradually becomes unable to eat more than a single and unhelpfully heavy meal a day, which has to be served at least eight hours before his bedtime. Describing a typical meal to a doctor, Proust details a menu of two eggs in a cream sauce, a wing of a roast chicken, three croissants, a plate of French fries, some grapes, some coffee and a bottle of beer.

— Digestion

'I go frequently – and badly – to the loo,' he tells the same doctor unsurprisingly. Constipation is quasi-permanent, relieved only by a strong laxative every two weeks, which usually brings on stomach cramps. As mentioned, urinating is no easier, it is accompanied by a sharp burning sensation, isn't possible often and the results display an excess of urea and uric acid: 'To ask pity of our body is like discoursing in front of an octopus, for which our words can have no more meaning than the sound of the tides.'

— Underpants

Needs to have these circling him tight around the stomach before he has any chance of getting to sleep. They have to be fastened by a special pin whose absence, when Proust accidentally loses it early one morning in the bathroom, keeps him awake all day.

— *Sensitive skin*

Can't use any soap, or cream or cologne. He has to wash with finely woven moistened towels, then pat himself dry with fresh linen [an average wash requires twenty towels, which Proust specifies must be taken to the only laundry which uses the right non-irritant powder, the blanchisserie Lavigne, which also does Jean Cocteau's laundry]. He finds that older clothes are better for him than new ones, and develops deep attachments to old shoes and handkerchiefs.

— *Mice*

Proust has a terror of these; when Paris is bombed by the Germans in 1918, he confides that he is more terrified of mice than cannons.

— *Cold*

Is always feeling it. Even in midsummer, he wears an overcoat and four jumpers if forced to leave the house. At dinner parties, he usually keeps a fur coat on. Nevertheless, people who greet him are surprised to find how cold his hands are. Fearing the effects of smoke, he doesn't allow his room to be properly heated, and keeps himself warm mostly through hot-water bottles and pullovers. It means he often has colds and, more particularly, a runny nose. At the end of one letter to Reynaldo Hahn, he mentions that he has wiped his nose eighty-three times since starting the letter. The letter is three pages long.

— Sensitivity to Altitude

On returning to Paris after visiting his uncle in Versailles, Proust experiences a malaise and is unable to climb the stairs to his apartment. In a letter to his uncle, he later attributes the problem to the change in altitude he has undergone. Versailles is eighty-three metres above Paris.

— Coughing

Does it very loudly. He reports of one fit in 1917: 'The neighbours, on hearing a continuous thundering and spasmodic barking, will think that I have bought either a church organ or a dog, or else that by some immoral (and purely imaginary) liaison with a lady, I have fathered a child who happens to have whooping cough.'

— Travel

Sensitive to any disruption of routine or habit, Proust suffers from homesickness and fears that every journey will kill him. He explains that in the first few days in a new place he is as unhappy as certain animals when night comes [it is not clear which animals he has in mind]. He formulates a wish to live on a yacht and thereby move around without having to get out of bed. He suggests this idea to the happily married Mme Straus: 'Would you like us to hire a boat in which there will be no noise and from which we shall watch all the most beautiful cities in the universe parade past us on the seashore without our leaving our bed (our beds)?' The proposal is not taken up.

— *Beds*
Loves his, spends most of his time in it, and turns it into his desk and office. Does the bed provide a defence against the cruel world outside? 'When one is sad, it is lovely to lie in the warmth of one's bed, and there, with all effort and struggle at an end, even perhaps with one's head under the blankets, surrender completely to wailing, like branches in the autumn wind.'

— *Noise From the Neighbours*
A manic sensitivity to it. Life in a Parisian block of flats is hellish, particularly when someone is doing a little music practice upstairs: 'There is an inanimate object which has a capacity to exasperate which no human being will ever attain: a piano.'

He is nearly killed by aggravation when redecoration starts in the flat adjoining his in the spring of 1907. He explains the problem to Mme Straus: the workmen arrive at seven in the morning, 'insist on manifesting their matinal high spirits by hammering ferociously and scraping their saws behind my bed, then idle for half an hour, then start hammering ferociously again so I can't get back to sleep . . . I'm at the end of my tether and my doctor advises me to go away because my condition is too serious to go on putting up with all this.' What is more, '(excuse me, Madame!) they are about to install a basin and a lavatory seat in her WC which is *next to* my bedroom wall'. And to finish him off: 'There's another gentleman who's moving in on the fourth floor of the same house, from which I can hear everything as though it was *in my bedroom*.' He resorts to calling his neighbour a cow, and when the workmen alter the size of her loo seat three times insinuates that it is to accommodate her enormous behind. Such is the noise, he concludes that there must be a Pharaonic dimension to the redecoration, and tells the keen Egyptologist Mme Straus: 'A dozen workers a day hammering away with such frenzy for so many months must have erected something as majestic as the Pyramid of Cheops which passers-by must be astonished to see between the Printemps and Saint-Augustin.' No pyramid is sighted.

— *Other Ailments*

'One thinks that people who are always ill don't also have the illnesses of other people,' Proust tells Lucien Daudet, 'but they do.' In this category, Proust includes fevers, colds, bad eyesight, an inability to swallow, toothache, elbow ache and dizziness.

— *Disbelief of Others*

Proust frequently has to suffer distressing insinuations that he is not as ill as he suggests. At the outbreak of the First World War the medical army board call him up for an examination. Though the man has been lying in bed more or less continuously since 1903, he is terrified that the severity of his illness will not be appropriately considered, and that he will be made to fight in the trenches. The prospect delights his stockbroker, Lionel Hauser, who sportingly tells Proust that he has not given up hope of one day seeing a Croix de Guerre on his chest. His client takes the idea badly: 'You know very well that in my state of health, I would be dead in forty-eight hours.' He is not called up.

A few years after the war, a critic accuses Proust of being a worldly fop, who self-indulgently lies in bed the entire day dreaming of chandeliers and grand ceilings, and only leaves his room at six in the evening to attend posh parties with nouveaux-riches types who would never buy his books. Enraged, Proust replies that he is an invalid, a man who is physically unable to get out of bed, either at six in the evening or at six in the morning, and is too ill even to walk around his own room [not even to open a window, he adds], let alone go to a party. A few months later, he nevertheless staggers to the opera.

— *Death*

Whenever he informs others of his health, Proust loses no time in declaring that he is about to die; he announces the fact with unwavering conviction and regularity for the last sixteen years of his life. He describes his customary state as 'suspended between caffeine, aspirin, asthma, angina pectoris and altogether between life and death every six days out of seven'.

Was he an extraordinary hypochondriac? His stockbroker,

Lionel Hauser, thought so, and eventually decided to be frank with him in a way that no one else had dared. 'Allow me to tell you,' he ventured, 'that even though you are approaching fifty, you've stayed what you were when I first knew you, namely a spoilt child. Oh, I know you're going to protest by seeking to show me that according to A + B − C, far from having been spoilt, you've always been a martyr child who no one has ever understood, but that is much more your fault than that of others.' If he had always been so ill, Hauser charged, the damage was largely self-inflicted, the result of staying in bed all the time with the curtains shut and thereby refusing the two constituents of health, sun and fresh air. In any case, with Europe engulfed in chaos after the First World War, Hauser urged Proust to take a little distance from his physical afflictions: 'You will have to admit that your health must be a lot better than that of Europe, even if it is still extremely precarious.'

Whatever the rhetorical power of the argument, Proust nevertheless succeeded in dying the following year.

Was Marcel exaggerating? The same virus can put one person to bed for a week, and only register in another as a mild drowsiness after lunch. Faced with someone who curls up in pain after scratching their finger, an alternative to condemning the theatrics is to imagine that this scratch may be experienced by the delicate-skinned creature as no less painful than a machete swing would be for us — and that we cannot therefore allow ourselves to judge the legitimacy of another's pain simply on the basis of the pain we would have suffered had we been similarly afflicted.

Proust was certainly delicate-skinned; Léon Daudet called him a man born without a skin. It can be hard to fall asleep after a copious meal. The digestive processes keep the body busy, the food lies heavy on the stomach, it seems more comfortable to be sitting up than lying down. But in Proust's case, the merest particle of food or liquid was enough to interrupt his sleep. He informed a doctor that he could drink a quarter of a glass of Vichy water before he went to bed, but that if he drank so much as a whole glass he would be kept awake by intolerable stomach pains. A confrère of the princess whose nights were ruined by a single pea, the author was cursed by a mystic's ability to detect every millilitre swilling in his intestinal sac.

Compare him to his brother, Robert Proust, two years younger than he, a surgeon like his father [the author of an acclaimed study of *The Surgery of the Female Genitalia*], and built like an ox. Whereas Marcel could be killed by a draught, Robert was indestructible. When he was nineteen he was riding a tandem bicycle in Reuil, a village on the Seine a few miles north of Paris. At a busy junction, he fell from his tandem and slipped under the wheels of an approaching five-ton coal wagon. The wagon rolled over him, he was rushed to hospital, his mother hurried from Paris in panic, but her son made a rapid and remarkable recovery, suffering none of the permanent damage the doctors had feared. When the First World War broke out, the ox, now a grown-up surgeon, was posted to a field hospital at Étain near Verdun, where he lived in a tent and worked in exhausting and unsanitary conditions. One day a shell landed on the hospital, and shrapnel scattered around the table where Robert was operating on a German soldier. Though hurt himself, Dr Proust single-handedly moved his patient to a nearby dormitory and continued the operation on a stretcher. A few years later he suffered a grave car accident when his driver fell asleep and the vehicle collided with an ambulance. Robert was thrown against a wooden partition, fractured his skull, but almost before his family had had time to be informed and grow alarmed, he was back on the road to recovery and active life.

So who would one wish to be, Robert or Marcel? The advantages of being the former can be briefly stated: immense physical energy, aptitude for tennis and canoeing, surgical skill [Robert was celebrated for his prostatectomies, an operation henceforth known in French medical circles as p*roust*atectomies], financial success, father of a beautiful daughter, Suzy [who uncle Marcel adored and spoilt, nearly buying her a flamingo when she expressed a passing desire for one as a child]. And Marcel? No physical energy, couldn't play tennis or canoe, made no money, had no children, enjoyed no respect until late in life, then felt too sick to derive any pleasure from it [a lover of analogies drawn from illness, he compared himself to a man afflicted with too high a fever to enjoy a perfect soufflé].

However, an area in which Robert appeared to trail his brother was in the ability to notice things. Robert didn't show much reaction when there was a window open on a pollen-rich day or five tons of coal had run over him: he could have travelled from Everest to Jericho and taken little note of an altitude change, or slept on five tins of peas without suspecting that there was anything unusual under the mattress.

Though such sensory blindness is often rather welcome, particularly when one is performing an operation during a shell barrage in the First World War, it is worth pointing out that feeling things [which usually means feeling them *painfully*] is at some level linked to the acquisition of knowledge. A sprained ankle quickly teaches us about the body's weight distribution, hiccups force us to notice and adjust to hitherto unknown aspects of the respiratory system, being jilted by a lover is a perfect introduction to the mechanisms of emotional dependency.

In fact, in Proust's view, we don't really learn anything properly until there is a problem, until we are in pain, until something fails to go as we had hoped:

> Infirmity alone makes us take notice and learn, and enables us to analyse processes which we would otherwise know nothing about. A man who falls straight into bed every night, and ceases to live until the moment when he wakes and rises, will surely never dream of making,

not necessarily great discoveries, but even minor observations about sleep. He scarcely knows that he is asleep.
A little insomnia is not without its value in making us
appreciate sleep, in throwing a ray of light upon that
darkness. An unfailing memory is not a very powerful
incentive to study the phenomena of memory.

Though we can of course use our minds without being in
pain, Proust's suggestion is that we become properly
inquisitive only when distressed. We suffer, therefore we
think, and we do so because thinking helps us to place pain
in context, it helps us to understand its origins, plot its
dimensions and reconcile ourselves to its presence.

It follows that ideas which have arisen without pain lack an
important source of motivation. For Proust, mental activity
seems divided into two categories: there are what might be
called *painless thoughts*, sparked by no particular discomfort,
inspired by nothing other than a disinterested wish to find
out how sleep works or why human beings forget; and
painful thoughts, arising out of a distressing inability to sleep
or recall a name – and it is this latter category which Proust
significantly privileges.

He tells us, for instance, that there are two methods by
which a person can acquire wisdom, painlessly via a teacher
or painfully via life, and he proposes that the painful variety
is the far superior; a point he places into the mouth of his

fictional painter Elstir, who treats the narrator to an argument in favour of making some mistakes:

> There is no man, however wise, who has not at some period of his youth said things, or even lived in a way which was so unpleasant to him in later life that he would gladly, if he could, expunge it from his memory. But he shouldn't regret this entirely, because he cannot be certain that he has indeed become a wise man – so far as any of us can be wise – unless he has passed through all the fatuous or unwholesome incarnations by which that ultimate stage must be reached. I know there are young people . . . whose teachers have instilled in them a nobility of mind and moral refinement from the very beginning of their schooldays. They perhaps have nothing to retract when they look back upon their lives; they can, if they choose, publish a signed account of everything they have ever said or done; but they are poor creatures, feeble descendants of doctrinaires, and their wisdom is negative and sterile. We cannot be taught wisdom, we have to discover it for ourselves by a journey which no one can undertake for us, an effort which no one can spare us.

Why can't they? Why is this painful journey so indispensable to the acquisition of true wisdom? Elstir does not specify, though it may be enough that he has defined a relation between the degree of pain a person experiences and the profundity of thought they may have as a result. It is as if the mind were a squeamish organ which refused to entertain difficult truths unless encouraged to do so by difficult events. 'Happiness is good for the body,' Proust tells us, 'but it is grief which develops the strengths of the mind.' These griefs put us through a form of mental gymnastics which we would have avoided in happier times. Indeed, if a genuine priority is the development of our mental capacities, the implication is that we would be better off being unhappy than content, better off pursuing tormented love affairs than reading Plato or Spinoza.

> A woman whom we need and who makes us suffer elicits from us a whole gamut of feelings far more profound and more vital than does a man of genius who interests us.

It is perhaps only normal if we remain ignorant when things are blissful. While a car is working well, what incentive is there to learn of its complex internal functioning? When a beloved pledges loyalty, why should we start to dwell on the dynamics of human treachery? What could encourage us to investigate the humiliations of social life when all we encounter is respect? Only when plunged into grief do we have the Proustian incentive to confront difficult truths, as we wail under the bedclothes, like branches in the autumn wind.

It may explain Proust's suspicion of doctors. Doctors are in an awkward position according to the Proustian theory of knowledge, for they are people who profess to understand the workings of the body, even though their knowledge has not primarily emerged from any pain in their *own* body. They have merely attended years of medical school.

It was the arrogance of this position which rankled the ever-ailing Proust, an arrogance all the more unfounded given the shaky foundations of medical knowledge in his day. As a child, he had been sent to see a certain Dr Martin, who claimed to have discovered a permanent cure for asthma. It involved burning off the erectile tissue of the nose in a two-hour-long session. 'You can go off to the countryside now,' an assured Dr Martin told young Proust after he had inflicted this painful operation on him, 'you *cannot* have hay fever any longer.' But, of course, at the first sight of a lilac in bloom, Proust was assaulted by such a violent, lengthy attack of asthma that his hands and feet turned purple and there were fears for his life.

The doctors in Proust's novel inspire little more confidence. When the narrator's grandmother is taken ill her worried family summon a renowned and celebrated medical figure, the Docteur du Boulbon. Though the grandmother is in extraordinary pain, du Boulbon conducts a rapid examination before deciding that he has hit upon the perfect solution.

> 'You will be cured, Madame, on the day, whenever it comes – and it rests entirely with you whether it comes today – on which you realize that there is nothing wrong with you and resume your ordinary life. You tell me that you have not been eating, not going out?'
>
> 'But, Doctor, I have a temperature.'
>
> 'Not just now at any rate. Besides, what a splendid excuse! Don't you know that we feed up tuberculosis

patients with temperatures of 102 and keep them out in the open air?'

Unable to resist the arguments of this exalted medical man, the grandmother forces herself out of bed, takes her grandson with her and painfully negotiates her way to the Champs-Élysées for the sake of fresh air. Naturally, the trip kills her.

Should a convinced Proustian ever visit a doctor? Marcel, the son and brother of surgeons, ended up with an equivo- cal, even surprisingly generous, verdict on the profession:

'To believe in medicine would be the height of folly, if not to believe in it were not a greater folly still.'

Proustian logic would nevertheless point to the wisdom of seeking out doctors who were themselves frequently afflicted by grave illness.

It now seems as if the magnitude of Proust's misfortunes should not be allowed to cast doubt on the validity of his ideas, indeed, it is the very extent of his suffering that we should take to be evidence of the perfect precondition for insights. It is when we hear that Proust's lover died in a plane crash off the coast of Antibes, that Stendhal endured a series of agonizing unrequited passions and that Nietzsche was a social outcast taunted by schoolboys, that we can be reassured of having discovered valuable intellectual authorities. It is not the contented or the glowing who have left many of the profound testimonies of what it means to be alive. It seems that such knowledge has usually been the privileged preserve of, and the only blessing granted to, the violently miserable.

Nevertheless, before subscribing uncritically to a Romantic cult of suffering, it should be added that suffering has, on its own, never been quite enough. It is unfortunately easier to lose a lover than complete *In Search of Lost Time*, to experience unrequited desire than write *De L'Amour*, to be socially unpopular than the author of *The Birth of Tragedy*. Many unhappy syphilitics omit to write their *Fleurs du Mal* and shoot themselves instead. Perhaps the greatest claim one can therefore make for suffering is that it opens up *possibilities* for intelligent, imaginative enquiry — possibilities which may quite easily be, and most often are, overlooked or refused.

How can we do neither? Even if the creation of a masterpiece plays no part in the ambition, how can we learn to suffer more successfully? Though philosophers have traditionally been concerned with the pursuit of happiness, far greater wisdom would seem to lie in pursuing ways to be properly and productively unhappy. The stubborn recurrence of misery means that the development of a workable approach to it must surely outstrip the value of any utopian quest for happiness. Proust, a veteran of grief, knew as much:

The whole art of living is to make use of the individuals through whom we suffer.

What would such an art of living involve? For a Proustian, the task is to gain a better understanding of reality. Pain is surprising: we cannot understand why we have been abandoned in love or left off an invitation list, why we are unable to sleep at night or wander through pollinating meadows in spring. Identifying reasons for such discomforts does not spectacularly absolve us of pain, but it may form the principal basis of a recovery. While assuring us that we are not uniquely cursed, understanding grants us a sense of the boundaries to, and bitter logic behind our suffering:

Griefs, at the moment when they change into ideas, lose some of their power to injure our heart.

However, only too frequently, suffering fails to alchemize into ideas, and instead of affording us a better sense of reality pushes us into a baneful direction where we learn nothing new, where we are subject to many more illusions and entertain far fewer vital thoughts than if we had never suffered to begin with. Proust's novel is filled with those we might call *bad sufferers*, wretched souls who have been betrayed in love, or excluded from parties, who are pained by a feeling of intellectual inadequacy or a sense of social inferiority but who learn nothing from such ills, and indeed react to them by engaging a variety of ruinous defence mechanisms, which entail arrogance and delusion, cruelty and callousness, spite and rage.

Without doing them an injustice, it may be possible to lift a number of these bad sufferers from the novel, so as to consider what is ailing them, the Proustian inadequacy of their defences, and to propose, in a gently therapeutic spirit, certain more fruitful responses.

Patient no. 1

Mme Verdurin: the bourgeois mistress of a salon that gathers to discuss art and politics, and which she calls her 'little clan'. Very much moved by art, she develops headaches when overcome by the beauty of music, and once dislocates her jaw by laughing too much.

Problem: Mme Verdurin has dedicated her life to rising in the social world, but she finds herself ignored by those she most desires to know. She is not on the invitation lists of the best aristocratic families, she would be unwelcome at the salon of the Duchesse de Guermantes, her own salon is filled only with members of her own social class and the President of the French Republic has never invited her to have lunch in the Élysée Palace – though he has invited Charles Swann, a man she considers to be no more elevated in the world than she is.

Response to problem: There are few outward signs that Mme Verdurin is bothered by her situation. She asserts with apparent conviction that anyone who refuses to invite her or come to her salon is merely a 'bore'. Even the President, Jules Grévy, is a bore.

The word is perversely appropriate, for it is the direct opposite of what Mme Verdurin in fact judges any grand figure to be. These figures excite her so much and yet are so inaccessible to her that all she can do is camouflage her disappointment in an unconvincing display of insouciance.

When Swann carelessly lets slip at the Verdurin salon that he is lunching with President Grévy the envy of the other guests is palpable, and, so as to dispel it, Swann quickly adopts a deprecating line:

> 'I assure you, his luncheon-parties are not in the least bit amusing. They're very simple affairs too, you know – never more than eight at table.'

Others might have recognized Swann's remark to be mere politeness, but Mme Verdurin is too distressed to ignore any suggestion that what she does not have is not worth having.

> 'I can easily believe that you don't find them amusing, those luncheons. Indeed, it's very good of you to go to them ... I've heard [the President] is as deaf as a post and eats with his fingers.'

A better solution: Why is Mme Verdurin suffering badly? Because we always lack more than we have, and because there are always more people who don't invite us than who do. Our sense of what is valuable will hence be radically distorted if we must perpetually condemn as tedious everything we lack, simply because we lack it.

How much more honest to hold in mind that, though we might like to meet the President, he doesn't want to meet us, but that this detail is no reason to reinvent our level of interest in him. Mme Verdurin might learn to understand the mechanisms by which people are excluded from social circles, she could learn to make light of her frustration, confess to it directly, even throw out a teasing remark to Swann asking him to return with a signed menu, and in the process, might become so charming that an invitation to the Élysée would make its way to her after all.

Patient no. 2

Françoise: who cooks for the narrator's family, producing wonderful asparagus and beef-in-jelly. She is also known for her stubborn personality, her cruelty towards the kitchen staff and her loyalty to her employers.

Problem: she doesn't know much. Françoise has never had any formal education, her knowledge of world affairs is scanty and she is badly acquainted with the political and royal events of her time.

Response to problem: Françoise has acquired a habit of suggesting that she knows everything. In short, she is a know-all, and her face registers the know-all's panic whenever she is informed of something that she has no clue about, though the panic is quickly suppressed so as to maintain composure:

> Françoise would refuse to appear surprised. You could have announced that the Archduke Rudolf, whom she had never suspected of existing, was not, as was generally supposed, dead, but alive and kicking, and she would only have answered, 'Yes,' as though she had known it all the time.

Psychoanalytic literature tells of a woman who felt faint whenever she sat in a library. Surrounded by books, she would develop nausea and could gain relief only by leaving their vicinity. It was not, as might be supposed, that she was averse to books, but rather that she wanted them and the knowledge they contained far too badly, that she felt her lack of knowledge far too strongly, wanted to have read everything on the shelves at once – and because she could not, needed to flee her unbearable ignorance by surrounding herself with a less knowledge-laden environment.

A precondition of becoming knowledgeable may be a resignation to, and accommodation with, the extent of one's ignorance, an accommodation which requires a sense that this ignorance need not be permanent, or indeed need not be taken personally, as a reflection of one's inherent capacities.

However, the know-all has lost faith in acquiring knowledge by legitimate means, which is perhaps not a surprising loss of faith in a character like Françoise, who has spent a lifetime cooking asparagus and beef-in-jelly for frighteningly well-educated employers, who have whole mornings to read the newspaper properly and are fond of wandering through the house quoting Racine and Mme de Sévigné – whose short stories she perhaps at some point claimed to have read.

A better solution: though Françoise's knowingness is a distorted reflection of a sincere desire for knowledge, Archduke Rudolf's true status will sadly remain a mystery until she accepts the momentary, painful loss of face required to ask who on earth this could be.

Patient no. 3

Alfred Bloch: a schoolfriend of the narrator; intellectual, bourgeois, Jewish, his appearance is compared to that of Sultan Mahomet II in Bellini's portrait.

Problem: prone to making gaffes and embarrassing himself on important occasions.

Response to problem: Bloch acts with extreme self-assurance where lesser mortals would offer humble apologies, experiencing no apparent shame or embarrassment.

The narrator's family invite him for dinner, for which he arrives an hour and a half late, covered with mud from head to toe because of an unexpected rain shower. He might have excused himself for the delay and muddy appearance, but Bloch says nothing, and instead launches into a speech expressing his disdain for the conventions of arriving clean and on time:

> 'I never allow myself to be influenced in the smallest degree either by atmospheric disturbances or by the arbitrary divisions of what is known as time. I would willingly reintroduce the use of the opium pipe or the Malay kris, but I know nothing about those infinitely more pernicious and moreover flatly bourgeois implements, the umbrella and the watch.'

It is not that Bloch has no wish to please. It simply seems that he cannot tolerate a situation where he has both tried to please and yet failed despite himself. How much easier, then, to offend and at least be in control of his actions. If he cannot be on time for dinner and is rained upon, why not turn the insults of time and meteorology into his own successes, declaring that he has willed the very things that have been inflicted on him?

A better solution: a watch, an umbrella, sorry.

Patient no. 4

She makes only a fleeting appearance in the novel. We don't know what colour her eyes are, how she dresses or what her full name is. She is merely known as the mother of Albertine's friend, Andrée.

Problem: like Mme Verdurin, Andrée's mother is concerned with rising in the social world. She wishes to be invited for dinner by the right people, and isn't. When her teenage daughter brings Albertine home, the girl innocently mentions that she has spent many holidays with the family of one of the governors of the Bank of France. This is striking news for Andrée's mother, who has never been graced with an invitation to their large house, and would love to have been.

Response to problem:

> Every evening at the dinner-table, while assuming an air of indifference and disdain, [Andrée's mother] was fascinated by Albertine's accounts of everything that had happened at the big house while she was staying there, and the names of the other guests, almost all of them people whom she knew by sight or by name. Even the thought that she knew them only in this indirect fashion ... gave Andrée's mother a touch of melancholy while she plied Albertine with questions about them in a lofty and distant tone, with pursed lips, and might have left her doubtful and uneasy as to the importance of her own social position had she not been able to reassure herself, to return safely to the 'realities of life', by saying to the butler, 'Please tell the chef that his peas aren't soft enough.' She then recovered her serenity.

The chef responsible for this serenity and these peas makes even less of an appearance in the novel than his boss. Should we call him Gérard or Joel? Is he from Brittany or the Languedoc, did he train as sous-chef at the Tour d'Argent or at the Café Voltaire? But the critical issue is why it had to become this man's problem that a governor of the Bank of France failed to invite his boss on holiday. Why did a bowl of his innocent peas have to carry the blame for the lack of an invitation to the governor's large house?

The Duchesse de Guermantes finds serenity in a similarly unfair and unenlightening way. The Duchesse has an unfaithful husband and a cold marriage. She also has a footman called Poullein, who is much in love with a young woman. Because this woman works as a servant in another household and her days off rarely coincide with Poullein's, the two lovers seldom meet. Shortly before one such longed-for meeting, a M. de Grouchy comes for dinner at the Duchesse's. During the meal, de Grouchy, a keen hunter, offers to send the Duchesse six brace of pheasants that he has shot on his country estate. The Duchesse thanks him, but insists that the gift is generous enough as it is, and that she will therefore send her own footman, Poullein, to pick up the pheasants, rather than further inconvenience M. de Grouchy and his staff. The fellow dinner guests are much impressed by the Duchesse's thoughtfulness. What they cannot know is that she has acted 'generously' for one reason only: so that Poullein will be unable to keep his appointment with his beloved, and so that the Duchesse will therefore be a little less troubled by evidence of romantic happiness which she has been denied in her own relationship.

A better solution: to spare the messenger, the cook, the footman, the peas.

Patient no. 5

Charles Swann: the man invited to lunch with the President, a friend of the Prince of Wales and an habitué of the most elegant salons. He is handsome, wealthy, witty, a little naive and very much in love.

Problem: Swann receives an anonymous letter saying that his lover, Odette, has in the past been the mistress of numerous men, and has often frequented brothels. A distraught Swann wonders who could possibly have sent him a letter with such hurtful revelations, and moreover notes that it contains details which only a personal acquaintance of his would know.

Response to problem: searching for the culprit, Swann considers each of his friends in turn; M. de Charlus, M. des Laumes, M. d'Orsan, but cannot believe this letter of any of them. Then, having been unable to suspect anyone, Swann begins to think more critically, and decides that everyone he knows could in fact have written the letter. What is he to think? How should he evaluate his friends? The cruel letter is an invitation for Swann to pursue a deeper understanding of people:

> This anonymous letter proved that he knew a human being capable of the most infamous conduct, but he could see no more reason why that infamy should lurk in the unfathomed depths of the character of the man with the warm heart rather than the cold, the artist rather than the bourgeois, the noble rather than the flunkey. What criterion ought one to adopt to judge human beings? After all, there was not a single person he knew who might not, in certain circumstances, prove capable of shameful action. Must he then cease to see them all? His mind grew clouded; he drew his hands two or three times across his brow, wiped his glasses with his handkerchief ... And he continued to shake hands with all the friends whom he had suspected, with the purely formal reservation that each one of them had possibly thought to drive him to despair.

A *better solution:* Swann has been made to suffer by the letter, but the suffering has led to no greater understanding. He may have shed a layer of sentimental innocence, he now knows that the surface behaviour of his friends may belie a darker interior, but he has found no way of identifying its signs or indeed its origins. His mind has grown clouded, he has wiped his glasses and he has missed out on what, for Proust, is the finest thing about betrayal and jealousy – its ability to generate the intellectual motivation necessary to investigate the hidden sides of others.

Though we sometimes suspect that people are hiding things from us, it is not until we are in love that we feel an urgency to push our enquiries, and in seeking answers we are apt to discover the extent to which people disguise and conceal their real lives.

It is one of the powers of jealousy to reveal to us the extent to which the reality of external facts and the emotions of the heart are an unknown element which lends itself to endless suppositions. We imagine that we know exactly what things are and people think, for the simple reason that we do not care about them. But as soon as we have a desire to know, as the jealous man has, then it becomes a kaleidoscope in which we can no longer distinguish anything.

Swann may know as a general truth that life is full of contrasts, but in the case of each person he knows he trusts that those parts of a life with which he is not familiar must be identical with the parts with which he is. He understands what is hidden from him in the light of what is revealed, and therefore understands nothing of Odette, difficult as it is to accept that a woman who seems so respectable when she is with him could be the same person who once frequented brothels. Similarly, he understands nothing of his friends, for it is hard to accept that someone with whom he entertained an amiable conversation at lunch could by dinner time have addressed a hurtful letter filled with crude revelations about his lover's past.

The lesson? To respond to the unexpected and hurtful

behaviour of others with something more than a wipe of the glasses, to see it as a chance to expand our understanding, even if, as Proust warns us, 'when we discover the true lives of other people, the real world beneath the world of appearance, we get as many surprises as on visiting a house of plain exterior which inside is full of hidden treasures, torture-chambers or skeletons'.

*

Compared to these unfortunate sufferers, Proust's approach to his own grief now seems rather admirable.

Though asthma made it life-threatening for him to spend time in the countryside, though he turned purple at the mere sight of a lilac in bloom, he resisted following the example of Mme Verdurin, he did not peevishly claim that flowers were boring or trumpet the advantages of spending the year in a shuttered room.

Though he had spectacular gaps in his knowledge, it was not beyond him to fill them. 'Who wrote *The Brothers Karamazov?*' he was asking Lucien Daudet [at the age of twenty-seven]. 'Has Boswelle's [sic] *Life of Johnson* [sic] been translated? And what's the best of Dickens (I haven't read anything)?'

Nor is there evidence that he redirected his disappointments onto his household staff. Having acquired a skill at turning grief into ideas, in spite of the state of his romantic life, when the driver he regularly used, Odilon Albaret, married the woman who would later become his maid,

Proust was able to respond with a telegram congratulating the couple on their special day, and did so with only the briefest burst of self-pity and the most modest attempt at guilt-induction, here highlighted in italics:

> Congratulations. I am not writing to you at greater length, *because I have caught a flu and I am tired*, but I send you all my deepest wishes for your happiness and that of your families.

The moral? To recognize that our best chance of contentment lies in taking up the wisdom offered to us in coded form through our coughs, allergies, social gaffes and emotional betrayals, and to avoid the ingratitude of those who blame the peas, the bores, the time and the weather.

CHAPTER FIVE

HOW TO EXPRESS
YOUR EMOTIONS

There may be significant things to learn about people by looking at what annoys them most. Proust got very annoyed by the way some people expressed themselves. Lucien Daudet tells us that Proust had a friend who thought it chic to use English expressions when he was speaking French, and would therefore say, 'Goodbye,' or, more casually, 'Bye, bye,' whenever he left a room. 'It made Proust positively unhappy,' reports Daudet, 'he would make the kind of pained, irritated grimace which follows when a stick of chalk has been scraped across a blackboard. "It really hurts your teeth, that kind of thing!" he would exclaim plaintively.' Proust displayed similar frustration with people who referred to the Mediterranean as 'the Big Blue', to England as 'Albion' and to the French Army as 'our boys'. He was pained by people whose sole response to heavy rain was, '*Il pleut des cordes*,' to cold weather, '*Il fait un froid de canard*,' and to another's deafness, '*Il est sourd comme un panier.*'

Why did these phrases affect Proust so much? Though the way people talk has altered somewhat since his day, it is not difficult to see that here were examples of rather poor expression, though if Proust was wincing, his complaint was more a psychological than a grammatical one ['No one knows less syntax than me,' he boasted]. Peppering French with bits of English, talking of Albion instead of England

and the Big Blue instead of the Mediterranean were signs of wishing to seem smart and in-the-know around 1900, and relying on essentially insincere, overelaborate stock phrases to do so. There was no reason to say 'bye, bye' when taking one's leave, other than a need to impress by recourse to a contemporary fad for all things British. And though phrases like '*Il pleut des cordes*' had none of the ostentation of a 'bye, bye', they were examples of the most exhausted constructions, whose use implied little concern for evoking the specifics of a situation. In so far as Proust made pained grimaces, it was in defence of a more honest and accurate approach to expression.

Lucien Daudet tells us how he first got a taste of it:

> One day when we were coming out of a concert where we had heard Beethoven's Choral symphony, I was humming some vague notes which I thought expressed the emotion I had just experienced, and I exclaimed, with an emphasis which I only later understood to be ridiculous: 'That's a wonderful bit!' Proust started to laugh and said, 'But, my dear Lucien, it's not your *poum, poum, poum* that's going to convey this wonderfulness! It would be better to try and explain it!' At the time, I wasn't very happy, but I had just received an unforgettable lesson.

It was a lesson in trying to find the right words for things. The process can be counted upon to go badly awry. We feel something, and reach out for the nearest phrase or hum with which to communicate, but which fails to do justice to what has induced us to do so. We hear Beethoven's Ninth and hum *poum, poum, poum*, we see the pyramids at Giza and go, 'That's nice.' These sounds are asked to account for an experience, but their poverty prevents either us or our interlocutors from really understanding what we have lived through. We stay on the outside of our impressions, as if staring at them through a frosted window, superficially related to them, yet estranged from whatever has eluded casual definition.

Proust had a friend called Gabriel de la Rochefoucauld. He was an aristocratic young man whose ancestor had written a famous short book in the seventeenth century, and who liked to spend time in glamorous Paris nightspots, so much time that he had been labelled by some of his more sarcastic contemporaries, 'le la Rochefoucauld de chez Maxim's'. But in 1904, Gabriel forsook the night life in order to try his hand at literature. The result was a novel, *The Lover and the Doctor*, which Gabriel sent to Proust in manuscript form as soon as it was finished, with a request for comments and advice.

'Bear in mind that you have written a fine and powerful novel, a superb, tragic work of complex and consummate craftsmanship,' Proust reported back to his friend, who might have formed a slightly different impression after reading the lengthy letter which had preceded this eulogy. It seems that the superb and tragic work had a few problems, not least because it was filled with clichés: 'There are some fine big landscapes in your novel,' explained Proust, treading delicately, 'but at times one would like them to be painted with more originality. It's quite true that the sky is on fire at sunset, but it's been said too often, and the moon that shines discreetly is a trifle dull.'

We may ask why Proust objected to phrases that had been used too often. After all, doesn't the moon shine discreetly? Don't sunsets look as if they were on fire? Aren't clichés just good ideas that have proved rightly popular?

The problem with clichés is not that they contain false ideas, but rather that they are superficial articulations of very good ones. The sun is often on fire at sunset and the moon discreet, but if we keep saying this every time we encounter a sun or a moon, we will end believing that this is the last rather than the first word to be said on the subject. Clichés are detrimental in so far as they inspire us to believe that they adequately describe a situation while merely grazing its surface. And if this matters, it is because the way we speak is ultimately linked to the way we feel, because how we *describe* the world must at some level reflect how we first *experience* it.

The moon Gabriel mentioned might of course have been discreet, but it was liable to have been a lot more besides. When the first volume of Proust's novel was published eight years after *The Lover and the Doctor*, one wonders whether Gabriel [if he wasn't back ordering Dom Perignon at

Maxim's] took time to notice that Proust had also included a moon, but that he had skirted two thousand years of ready-made moon talk, and uncovered an unusual metaphor better to capture the reality of the lunar experience.

> Sometimes in the afternoon sky a white moon would creep up like a little cloud, furtive, without display, suggesting an actress who does not have to 'come on' for a while, and so goes 'in front' in her ordinary clothes to watch the rest of the company for a moment, but keeps in the background, not wishing to attract attention to herself.

Even if we recognize the virtues of Proust's simile, it is not necessarily one we could easily come up with by ourselves. It may lie closer to a genuine impression of the moon, but if we observe the moon and are asked to say something about it, we are more likely to hit upon a tired rather than an inspired image. We may be well aware that our description of a moon is not up to the task, without knowing how to better it. To take licence with his response, this would perhaps have bothered Proust less than an unapologetic use of clichés by people who believed that it was always right to follow verbal conventions ['golden orb', 'heavenly body'], and who felt that a priority when talking was not to be original but to sound like someone else.

Wanting to sound like other people has its temptations. There are inherited habits of speech guaranteed to make us sound authoritative, intelligent, worldly, appropriately grateful or deeply moved. As of a certain age, Albertine decides that she too would like to speak like someone else; like a bourgeois young woman. She begins to use a range of expressions common among such women, which she has picked up from her aunt, Mme Bontemps, in the slavish way, Proust suggests, that a baby goldfinch learns how to act like a grown-up by imitating the behaviour of its parent goldfinches. She acquires a habit of repeating whatever one says to her, so as to appear interested and in the process of forming an opinion of her own. If you tell her that an artist's work is good, or his house nice, she will say, 'Oh, his painting's good, is it?' 'Oh, his house is nice, is it?' Furthermore, when she meets someone unusual, she now says, 'He's a character,' when you suggest a game of cards to her, she will say, 'I don't have money to burn,' when one of her friends reproaches her unjustly, she will exclaim, 'You really are the limit!', all these expressions having been dictated to her by what Proust calls a 'bourgeois tradition almost as old as the *Magnificat* itself', a tradition laying down speech codes which the respectable bourgeois girl must learn, 'just as she has learned to say her prayers and to curtsy'.

This mockery of Albertine's verbal habits explains Proust's particular frustration with Louis Ganderax.

Louis Ganderax was a leading early-twentieth-century man of letters and the literary editor of the *Revue de Paris*. In 1906, he was asked to edit the correspondence of Georges Bizet, and to write a preface for the collection. It was a great honour, and a great responsibility. Bizet, who had died some thirty years earlier, was a composer of worldwide significance, whose place in posterity was assured by his opera, *Carmen*, and his Symphony in C Major. There was understandable pressure on Ganderax to produce a preface worthy of standing at the head of a genius's correspondence.

Georges Bizet

Unfortunately, Ganderax was something of a goldfinch and in an attempt to sound grand, far grander than he must have thought himself naturally to be, he ended up writing a preface of immense, almost comic pretension.

Lying in bed reading the newspaper in the autumn of 1908, Proust landed on an extract of Ganderax's preface, whose prose style annoyed him so much that he exorcised his feelings by writing a letter to Georges Bizet's widow, his good friend Mme Straus.

Louis Ganderax

'Why, when he can write so well, does he write as he does?' wondered Proust. 'Why, when one says "1871", add "that most abominable of all years"? Why is Paris immediately dubbed "the great city" and Delaunay "the master painter"? Why must emotion inevitably be "discreet" and good-naturedness "smiling" and bereavements "cruel", and countless other fine phrases that I can't remember?'

These phrases were of course anything but fine, they were a caricature of fineness, they were phrases that might once have been impressive in the hands of classical writers, but were pompous ornamentation when stolen by an author of a later age concerned only to suggest literary grandeur.

If Ganderax had worried about the sincerity of what he was saying, he might have resisted capping the thought that 1871 was a bad year with the melodramatic claim that it was in fact 'that most abominable of all years'. Paris might have been under siege by the Prussian army at the beginning of 1871, the starving populace might have been driven to eat elephants from the Jardin des Plantes, the Prussians might have marched down the Champs-Élysées and the Commune imposed tyrannical rule, but did these experiences really stand a chance of being conveyed in an overblown, thunderous phrase like this?

But Ganderax hadn't written nonsensical fine phrases by mistake. It was the natural outcome of his ideas on how people should express themselves. For Ganderax, the priority of good writing was to follow precedent, to follow examples of the most distinguished authors in history, while bad writing began with the arrogant belief that one could avoid paying homage to great minds and write according to one's fancy. It was fitting that Ganderax had elsewhere awarded himself the title of 'Defender of the French Language'. The language needed to be protected against the assaults of decadents who refused to follow the rules of expression dictated by tradition, leading Ganderax to complain publicly if he spotted a past participle in the wrong place or a word falsely applied in a published text.

Proust couldn't have disagreed more with such a view of tradition, and let Mme Straus know it:

Every writer is obliged to create his own language, as
every violinist is obliged to create his own 'tone' ... I
don't mean to say that I like original writers who write
badly. I prefer – and perhaps it's a weakness – those who
write well. But they begin to write well only on
condition that they're original, that they create their own
language. Correctness, perfection of style do exist, but
on the other side of originality, after having gone
through all the faults, not this side. Correctness this side
– 'discreet emotion', 'smiling good nature', 'most abominable of all years' – doesn't exist. The only way to
defend language is to attack it, yes, yes, Madame Straus!

Ganderax had overlooked the way that every good writer in
history, a history he so strongly wished to defend, had, in
order to assure adequate expression, broken a range of rules
laid down by previous writers. If Ganderax had been alive
in Racine's day, Proust mockingly imagined that the
Defender of the Language would have told even this
embodiment of classical French that he couldn't write very
well, because Racine had written slightly differently from
those before him. He wondered what Ganderax would have
made of Racine's lines in *Andromaque*:

> I loved you fickle; faithful, what might I have done? . . .
> Why murder him? What did he? By what right?
> Who told you to?

Pretty enough, but didn't these lines break important laws
of grammar? Proust pictured Ganderax delivering a rebuke
to Racine:

I understand your thought; you mean that since I loved you when you were fickle, what might that love have been if you had been faithful. But it's badly expressed. It could equally well mean that *you* would have been faithful. As official defender of the French language, I cannot let that pass.

'I'm not making fun of your friend, madame, I assure you,' claimed Proust, who hadn't stopped ridiculing Ganderax since the start of his letter. 'I know how intelligent and learned he is. It's a question of "doctrine". This man who is so sceptical has grammatical certainties. Alas, Madame Straus, there are no certainties, even grammatical ones . . . only that which bears the imprint of our choice, our taste, our uncertainty, our desire and our weakness can be beautiful.'

And a personal imprint is not only more beautiful, it is also a good deal more authentic. Trying to sound like Chateaubriand or Victor Hugo when you are in fact the literary editor of the *Revue de Paris* implies a singular lack of concern with capturing what is distinctive about being Louis Ganderax, much as attempting to sound like the archetypal bourgeois Parisian young woman ['I don't have money to burn', 'You really are the limit!'] when you are in fact a particular young woman called Albertine involves flattening your identity to fit a constrained social envelope. If, as Proust suggests, we are obliged to create our own language, it is because there are dimensions to ourselves absent from clichés, which require us to flout etiquette in order to convey with greater accuracy the distinctive timbre of our thought.

The need to lay a personal imprint on language is rarely more evident than in the personal sphere. The better we know someone the more the standard name they bear comes to seem inadequate, and the greater the desire to twist it into a new one, so as to reflect our awareness of their particularities. Proust's name on his birth certificate was Valentin Louis Georges Eugène Marcel Proust, but because this was a dry mouthful it was appropriate that those closest to him moulded it into something more suited to who Marcel was for them. For his beloved mother, he was *mon petit jaunet* [my little yellow one], or *mon petit serin* [my little canary], or *mon petit benêt* [my little clod] or *mon petit nigaud* [my little oaf]. He was also known as *mon pauvre loup* [my poor wolf], *petit pauvre loup* [poor little wolf] and *le petit loup* [the little wolf – Mme Proust called Marcel's brother Robert *mon autre loup*, which gives us a sense of family priorities]. To his friend Reynaldo Hahn, Proust was 'Buncht' [and Reynaldo 'Bunibuls'], to his friend Antoine Bibesco, Proust was 'Lecram' and when he got too friendly, *le Flagorneur* [the toady], or not straight enough, *le Saturnien*. At home, he wanted his maid to know him as 'Missou' and he would call her 'Plouplou'.

If Missou, Buncht and the *petit jaunet* are endearing symbols of the way new words and phrases can be constructed to capture new dimensions of a relationship, then confusing Proust's name with someone else's looks like a sadder symbol of a reluctance to expand a vocabulary to account for the variety of the human species. To people who didn't know Proust very well, rather than making his name more personal they had a depressing tendency to give him another name altogether, that of a far more famous contemporary writer, Marcel Prévost. 'I am totally unknown,' specified Proust in 1912. 'When readers write to me at *Le Figaro* after an article, which happens rarely, the letters are forwarded to Marcel Prévost, for whom my name seems to be no more than a misprint.'

Using a single word to describe two different things [the author of *In Search of Lost Time* and the author of *The Strong Virgins*] suggests a disregard for the world's real diversity that bears comparison with that shown by the cliché user. A person who invariably describes heavy rain with the phrase '*il pleut des cordes*' can be accused of neglecting the real diversity of rain showers, much as the person who calls every writer whose name begins with *P* and ends in *t* Monsieur Prévost can be accused of neglecting the real diversity of literature.

So if speaking in clichés is problematic, it is because the world itself contains a far broader range of rainfalls, moons, sunshines and emotions than stock expressions either capture or teach us to expect.

Proust's novel is filled with people who behave in un-stock ways. It is, for example, a conventional belief about family life that old aunts who love their family will entertain benevolent daydreams about them. But Proust's aunt Léonie loves her family greatly, and it doesn't stop her from deriving pleasure in involving them in the most macabre scenarios. Confined to her bed on account of a host of imaginary ailments, she is so bored with life that she longs for something exciting to happen to her, even if it should be something terrible. The most exciting thing she can imagine is a fire that would leave no stone of her house standing and would kill her entire family, but from which she herself would have plenty of time to escape. She would then be able to mourn her family affectionately for many years, and cause universal stupefaction in her village by getting out of bed to conduct the obsequies, crushed but courageous, moribund but erect.

Aunt Léonie would no doubt have preferred to die under torture than admit to harbouring such 'unnatural' thoughts – which does nothing to stop them from being very normal, if only rarely discussed.

Albertine has some comparably normal thoughts. She walks into the narrator's room one morning and experiences a rush of affection for him. She tells him how clever he is, and swears that she would rather die than leave him. If we asked Albertine why she had suddenly felt this rush of affection, one imagines her pointing to her boyfriend's intellectual or spiritual qualities – and we would of course be inclined to believe her, for this is a dominant societal interpretation of the way affection is generated.

However, Proust quietly lets us know that the real reason why Albertine feels so much love for her boyfriend is that he has had a very close shave this morning, and that she adores smooth skin. The implication is that his cleverness counts for little in her particular enthusiasm; if he refused to shave ever again, she might leave him tomorrow.

This is an inopportune thought. We like to think of love as arising from more profound sources. Albertine might vigorously deny that she had ever felt love because of a close shave, accuse you of perversion for suggesting it and attempt to change the subject. It would be a pity. What can replace a clichetic explanation of our functioning is not an image of perversity, but a broader conception of what is normal. If Albertine accepted that her reactions only demonstrated that a feeling of love can have an extraordinary range of origins, some more valid than others, then she might calmly evaluate the foundations of her relationship and identify the role which she wished good shaving to play in her emotional life.

In his descriptions both of aunt Léonie and Albertine, Proust offers us a picture of human behaviour that initially fails to match an orthodox account of how people operate, though it may in the end be judged to be a far *more* truthful picture than the one it has challenged.

The structure of this process may, rather obliquely, shed light on why Proust was so attracted to the story of the Impressionist painters.

In 1872, the year after Proust was born, Claude Monet exhibited a canvas entitled *Impression, Sunrise*. It depicted the harbour of Le Havre at dawn, and allowed viewers to discern, through a thick morning mist and a medley of unusually choppy brush strokes, the outline of an industrial seafront, with an array of cranes, smoking chimneys and buildings.

Impression: Sunrise, Claude Monet

The canvas looked a bewildering mess to most who saw it, and particularly irritated the critics of the day, who pejoratively dubbed its creator and the loose group to which he belonged 'impressionists', indicating that Monet's control of the technical side of painting was so limited that all he had been able to achieve was a childish daubing, bearing precious little resemblance to what dawns in Le Havre really looked like.

The contrast with the judgement of the art establishment a few years later could of course hardly have been greater. It seemed that not only could the Impressionists use a brush after all, but that their technique was masterful at capturing a dimension of visual reality overlooked by less talented contemporaries. What could explain such a dramatic reappraisal? Why had Monet's Le Havre been a great mess then a remarkable representation of a Channel port?

The Proustian answer starts with the idea that we are all in the habit of,

> giving to what we feel a form of expression which differs so much from, and which we nevertheless after a little time take to be, reality itself.

In this view, our *notion* of reality is at variance with actual reality, because it is so often shaped by inadequate or misleading accounts. Because we are surrounded by clichéd depictions of the world, our initial response to Monet's *Impression, Sunrise* may well be to baulk and complain that

Le Havre looks nothing like that, much as our initial response to aunt Léonie's and Albertine's behaviour may be to think that this comportment lacks any possible basis in reality. If Monet is a hero in this scenario, it is because he has freed himself from traditional, and in some ways limited, representations of Le Havre, in order to attend more closely to his own, uncorrupted impressions of the scene.

In a form of homage to the Impressionist painters, Proust inserted one into his novel, the fictional Elstir, who shares traits with Renoir, Degas and Manet. In the seaside resort of Balbec, Proust's narrator visits Elstir's studio, where he finds canvases which, like Monet's Le Havre, challenge the orthodox understanding of what things look like. In Elstir's seascapes, there is no demarcation between the sea and the sky, the sky looks like the sea, the sea like the sky. In a painting of a harbour at Carquethuit, a ship which is out at sea seems to be sailing through the middle of the town, women gathering shrimps among the rocks look as if they were in a marine grotto overhung by ships and waves, a group of holidaymakers in a boat look like they were in a carriole riding up through sunlit fields and down through shady patches.

Elstir is not trying his hand at surrealism. If his work seems unusual, it is because he is attempting to paint something of what we *actually see* when we look around, rather than what we *know we see*. We know that ships don't sail through the middle of towns, but it can sometimes look as if this is happening when we see a ship against the backdrop of a town from a certain light at a certain angle. We know there is a demarcation between the sea and the sky, but it can on occasion be hard to tell whether an azure-coloured band is in fact part of the sea or the sky, the confusion lasting only until our reason re-establishes a distinction between the two elements which had been missing from our first glance. Elstir's achievement is to hang on to the original muddle, and to set down in paint a visual impression before it has been overruled by what he knows.

Proust was not implying that painting had reached its apotheosis in Impressionism, and that the movement had triumphantly captured 'reality' in a way that previous schools of art had not. His appreciation of painting ranged further than this, but the works of Elstir illustrated with particular clarity what is arguably present in every success-ful work of art: an ability to restore to our sight a distorted or neglected aspect of reality. As Proust expressed it:

> Our vanity, our passions, our spirit of imitation, our abstract intelligence, our habits have long been at work, and it is the task of art to undo this work of theirs, making us travel back in the direction from which we have come to the depths where what has really existed lies unknown within us.

And what lies unknown within us includes such surprising things as ships that go through towns, seas that are momentarily indistinguishable from skies, fantasies that our beloved family will die in a major conflagration and intense feelings of love sparked by contact with smooth skin.

The moral? That life can be a stranger substance than clichéd life, that goldfinches should occasionally do things differently from their parents, and that there are persuasive reasons for calling a loved one Plouplou, Missou or poor little wolf.

CHAPTER SIX

HOW TO BE
A GOOD FRIEND

What did his friends think of him? He had a great number of them, and after his death many were moved to publish accounts of what it had been like to know him. The verdict could hardly have been more favourable. They were almost unanimous in suggesting that Proust had been a paragon of companionship, an embodiment of friendship's every virtue.

Their accounts tell us:

— *That he was generous*

'I can still see him, wrapped in his fur coat, even in springtime, sitting at a table in Larue's restaurant, and I can still see the gesture of his delicate hand as he tried to make you let him order the most extravagant supper, accepting the head waiter's biased suggestions, offering you champagne, exotic fruits and grapes on their vine-plant which he had noticed on the way in . . . He told you there was no better way of proving your friendship than by accepting.' – Georges de Lauris

— *That he was munificent*

'In restaurants, and everywhere where there was a chance, Marcel would give enormous tips. This was the case even in the slightest railway station buffet where he would never return.' – Georges de Lauris

— *That he liked to add a 200% service charge*

'If a dinner cost him ten francs, he would add twenty francs for the waiter.' – Fernand Gregh

— That he was not merely exorbitant

'The legend of Proust's generosity should not develop to the detriment of that of his goodness.' – Paul Morand

— That he didn't talk only about himself

'He was the best of listeners. Even in his intimate circle his constant care to be modest and polite prevented him from pushing himself forward and from imposing subjects of conversation. These he found in others' thoughts. Sometimes he spoke about sport and motor cars and showed a touching desire for information. He took an interest in you, instead of trying to make you interested in himself.' – Georges de Lauris

— That he was curious

'Marcel was passionately interested in his friends. Never have I seen less egoism, or egotism . . . He wanted to amuse you. He was happy to see others laughing and he laughed.' – Georges de Lauris

— That he didn't forget what was important

'Never, right up to the end, neither his frenzied work nor his suffering made him forget his friends – because he certainly never put all his poetry into his books, he put as much into his life.' – Walter Berry

— That he was modest

'What modesty! You apologized for everything: for being present, for speaking, for being quiet, for thinking, for expressing your dazzlingly meandering thoughts, even for lavishing your incomparable praise.' – Anna de Noailles

— That he was a great talker

'One can never say it enough: Proust's conversation was dazzling, bewitching.' – Marcel Plantevignes

— *That one never got bored at his house*
'During dinner, he would carry his plate over to each guest; he would eat soup next to one, the fish, or half a fish besides another, and so on until the end of a meal; one can imagine that by the fruit he had gone all the way around. It was testimony of kindness, of good-will towards everyone, because he would have been distraught that anyone would have wanted to complain; and he thought both to make a gesture of individual politeness and to assure, with his usual perspicacity, that everyone was in an agreeable mood. Indeed, the results were excellent, and one never got bored at his house.' – Gabriel de la Rochefoucauld

Given such generous verdicts, it is surprising to find that Proust held some extremely caustic views about friendship, in fact, to find that he had an unusually limited conception of the value of his, or indeed, of anyone's friendships. Despite the dazzling conversation and dinner parties, he believed:

— *That he could just as well have befriended a settee*
'The artist who gives up an hour of work for an hour of conversation with a friend knows that he is sacrificing a reality for something that does not exist (our friends being friends only in the light of an agreeable folly which travels with us through life and to which we readily accommodate ourselves, but which at the bottom of our hearts we know to be no more reasonable than the delusion of the man who talks to the furniture because he believes that it is alive).'

   — That talking is a futile activity
'Conversation, which is friendship's mode of expression, is a superficial digression which gives us nothing worth acquiring. We may talk for a lifetime without doing more than indefinitely repeat the vacuity of a minute.'
   — That friendship is a shallow effort
'. . . directed towards making us sacrifice the only part of ourselves that is real and incommunicable (otherwise than by means of art) to a superficial self.'
   — And that friendship is in the end no more than
'. . . a lie which seeks to make us believe that we are not irremediably alone.'

It doesn't mean he was callous. It doesn't mean he was a misanthrope. It doesn't mean he lacked the urge to see friends [an urge he described as a 'craving to see people which attacks both men and women and inspires a longing to throw himself out of the window in the patient who has been shut away from his family and friends in an isolation clinic'].

However, Proust *was* challenging all the more exalted claims made on friendship's behalf. Principal among these is the claim that our friends afford us a chance to express our deepest selves, and that the conversations we have with them are a privileged forum in which to say what we really think, and, by extension and with no mystical allusion, be who we really are.

The claim was not dismissed out of an embittered regret for the calibre of his friends. Proust's scepticism had nothing to do with the presence at his dinner table of intellectually sluggish characters like Gabriel de la Rochefoucauld, who needed to be entertained while he circulated with a half-eaten plate of fish in his hand. The problem was more universal, it was inherent within the idea of friendship and would have been present even if he had had a chance to share his thoughts with the most profound minds of his generation, even if he had, for instance, been given the opportunity to converse with a writer of James Joyce's genius.

Which in fact he did. In 1922, both writers were at a black-tie dinner given at the Ritz for Stravinsky, Diaghilev and members of the Russian Ballet, in order to celebrate the first night of Stravinsky's *Le Renard*. Joyce arrived late and without a dinner jacket, Proust kept his fur coat on throughout the evening and what happened once they were introduced was later reported by Joyce to a friend:

> Our talk consisted solely of the word 'Non.' Proust asked me if I knew the duc de so-and-so. I said, 'Non.' Our hostess asked Proust if he had read such and such a piece of *Ulysses*. Proust said, 'Non.' And so on.

After dinner, Proust got into his taxi with his hosts, Violet and Sydney Schiff, and without asking, Joyce followed them in. His first gesture was to open the window and his second to light a cigarette, both of which were life-threatening acts as far as Proust was concerned. During the journey, Joyce watched Proust without saying a word, while Proust talked continuously and failed to address a word to Joyce. When they arrived at Proust's flat at the Rue Hamelin, Proust took Sydney Schiff aside and said: 'Please ask Monsieur Joyce to let my taxi drive him home.' The taxi did so. The two men were never to meet again.

If the story has its absurd side, it is because of an awareness of what these two writers *could* have told one another. A conversation of culs-de-sac ending in 'Non' is not a surprising eventuality for many, it is more surprising and far more regrettable when it is all that the authors of *Ulysses* and *In Search of Lost Time* can find to say to one other when they are seated together under the same Ritz chandelier.

However, imagine that the evening had unfolded more successfully, as successfully as could have been hoped:

Proust: [*while taking furtive stabs at an* homard à l'américaine, *huddled in his fur coat*] Monsieur Joyce, do you know the Duc de Clermont-Tonnerre?
Joyce: Please, *appelez-moi* James. Le Duc! What a close and excellent friend, the kindest man I have met from here to Limerick.
Proust: Really? I am so glad we agree [*beaming at the discovery of this common acquaintance*], though I have not yet been to Limerick.

Violet Schiff: [*leaning across, with a hostess's delicacy, to Proust*] Marcel, do you know James's big book?

Proust: *Ulysses? Naturellement.* Who has not read the masterpiece of our new century?

[*Joyce blushes modestly, but nothing can disguise his delight*]

Violet Schiff: Do you remember any passages in it?

Proust: Madame, I remember the entire book. For instance, when the hero goes to the library, excuse my accent anglais, but I cannot resist: [*starting to quote*] 'Urbane, to comfort them, the Quaker librarian purred . . .'

And yet, even if it had gone as well as this, even if they had later enjoyed an animated cab ride home and sat up until sunrise exchanging thoughts on music and the novel, art and nationality, love and Shakespeare, there would still have been a critical discrepancy between the conversation and the work, between the chat and the writing, for *Ulysses* and *In Search of Lost Time* would never have resulted from a dialogue, even though these novels were among the most profound and sustained utterances both men were capable of – a point which highlights the limitations of conversation, when viewed as a forum in which to express our deepest selves.

What explains such limitations? Why would one be unable to chat, as opposed to write at the level of *In Search of Lost Time*? In part, because of the mind's functioning, its condition as an intermittent organ, forever liable to lose the thread or be distracted, generating vital thoughts only between stretches of inactivity or mediocrity, stretches in which we are not really 'ourselves', during which it may be no exaggeration to say that we are not quite all there as we gaze at passing clouds with a vacant, childlike expression. Because the rhythm of a conversation makes no allowance for dead periods, because the presence of others calls for continuous responses, we are left to regret the inanity of what we say, and the missed opportunity of what we do not.

By contrast, a book provides for a distillation of our sporadic minds, a record of its most vital manifestations, a concentration of inspired moments that might originally have arisen across a multitude of years, and been separated by extended stretches of bovine gazing. To meet an author whose books one has enjoyed must, in this view, necessarily be a disappointment ['It's true that there are people who are superior to their books, but that's because their books are not *Books*'], because such a meeting can only reveal a person as they exist within, and find themselves subject to the limitations of time.

Furthermore, conversation allows us little room to revise our original utterances, which ill suits our tendency not to know what we are trying to say until we have had at least one go at saying it; whereas writing accommodates and is largely made up of rewriting, during which original thoughts – bare inarticulate strands – are enriched and nuanced over time. They may thereby appear on a page according to the logic and aesthetic order *they* demand, as opposed to suffering the distortion effected by conversation, with its limits on the corrections or additions one can make before enraging even the most patient companion.

Proust famously did not realize the nature of what he was trying to write until he had begun to write it. When the first volume of *In Search of Lost Time* was published in 1913, there was no thought of the work assuming the gargantuan proportions it eventually did; Proust projected that it would be a trilogy [*Swann's Way, The Guermantes Way, Time Regained*], and even hoped the last two parts would fit into a single volume.

However, the First World War radically altered the plans by delaying the publication of the succeeding volume by four years, during which time Proust discovered a host of new things he wanted to say, and realized that he would require a further four volumes to say it. The original five hundred thousand words expanded to more than a million and a quarter.

It was not just the overall shape of the novel that changed. Each page, and a great many sentences, grew, or were altered in the passage from initial expression to printed form. Half of the first volume was rewritten four times. As Proust went back over what he had written he repeatedly recognized the imperfections of his initial attempt, words or parts of sentences were eliminated, points that he had

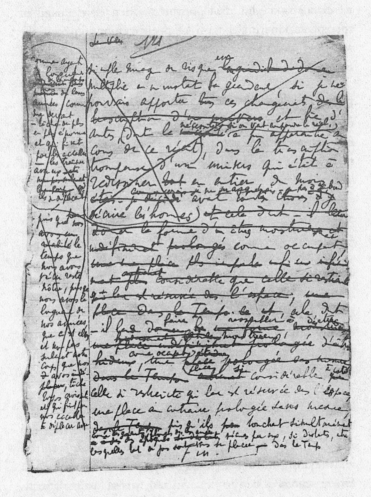

judged complete seemed to be crying out for recomposition, or elaboration and development with a new image or metaphor. Hence the mess of the manuscript pages, the result of a mind perpetually improving on its original utterances.

Unfortunately for Proust's publishers, the revisions did not cease once he had sent his handwritten scrawls to be typed up. The publishers' proofs, in which the scrawl found itself turned into elegant uniform letters, only served to reveal yet more errors and omissions, which Proust would correct in illegible bubbles, expanding into every stretch of white space available until, at times, they overflowed into narrow paper flaps glued onto the edge of the sheet.

It might have enraged the publisher, but it served to make a better book. It meant that the novel could be the product of the efforts of more than a single Proust [which any interlocutor would have had to be satisfied with], it was the product of a succession of ever more critical and accomplished authors [three at the very minimum; Proust[1] who had written the manuscript + Proust[2] who reread it + Proust[3] who corrected the proofs]. There was naturally no sign of the process of elaboration or of the material conditions of creation in the published version, only a continuous, controlled, faultless voice, revealing nothing of where sentences had to be rewritten, where asthma attacks had intruded, where a metaphor had to be altered, where a point had to be clarified and between which lines the author

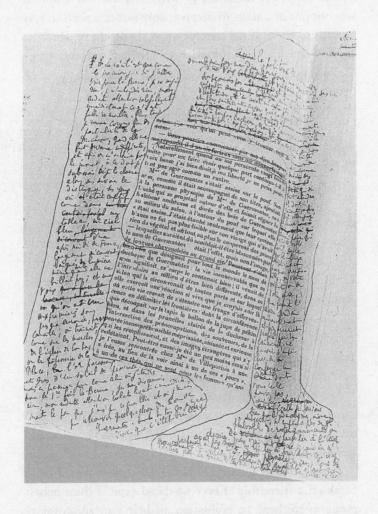

had to sleep, eat breakfast or write a thank-you letter. It was not out of a wish to deceive, only out of a wish to stay faithful to the original conception of the work, in which an asthma attack or a breakfast, though part of the author's life, had no place in the conception of the work, because, as Proust saw it:

> A book is the product of another self to the one we display in our habits, in society, in our vices.

*

In spite of its limitations as a forum in which to express complex ideas in rich, precise language, friendship could still be defended on the grounds that it provides us with a chance to communicate our most intimate, honest thoughts to people, and for once, reveal exactly what is on our minds.

Though an appealing notion, the likelihood of such honesty seems highly dependent on two things:

Firstly: how much is on our minds; in particular, how many thoughts we have about our friends which, though true, could potentially be hurtful, and though honest, could seem unkind.

Secondly: our evaluation of how ready others would be to break off a friendship if ever we dared express these honest thoughts to them, an evaluation made in part according to our sense of how loveable we are, and of whether our qualities would be enough to ensure that we could stay friends with people even if we had momentarily irritated them by revealing our disapproval of their fiancée or lyric poetry.

Unfortunately, by both criteria Proust was not well placed to enjoy honest friendships. For a start, he had far too many true but unkind thoughts about people. When he met a palm reader in 1918, the woman was said to have taken a glance at his hand, looked at his face for a moment, then remarked simply, 'What do you want from me, Monsieur? It should be you reading *my* character.' But this miraculous understanding of others did not lead to cheerful conclusions. 'I feel infinite sadness at seeing how few people are genuinely kind,' he said, and judged that most people had something rather wrong with them:

> The most perfect person in the world has a certain defect which shocks us or makes us angry. One man is of rare intelligence, sees everything from the loftiest viewpoint, never speaks ill of anyone, but will pocket and forget letters of supreme importance which he himself asked you to let him post for you, and so makes you miss a vital engagement without offering you any excuse, with a smile, because he prides himself upon never knowing the time. Another is so refined, so gentle, so delicate in his conduct that he never says anything to you about yourself that you would not be glad to hear, but you feel that he suppresses, that he keeps buried in his heart, where they turn sour, other, quite different opinions.

Lucien Daudet felt that Proust possessed:

> an unenviable power of divination, he discovered all the
> pettiness, often hidden, of the human heart, and it
> horrified him: the most insignificant lies, the mental
> reservations, the secrecies, the fake disinterestedness,
> the kind word which has an ulterior motive, the truth
> which has been slightly deformed for convenience, in
> short, all the things which worry us in love, sadden us
> in friendship and make our dealings with others banal
> were for Proust a subject of constant surprise, sadness or
> irony.

It is regrettable, as far as the cause of honest friendship was
concerned, that Proust combined this heightened awareness
of others' faults with unusually strong doubts about his
own chances of being liked ['Oh! Making a nuisance of
myself, that has always been my nightmare'], and about the
chances of retaining his friends if ever he were to express
his more negative thoughts to them. His previously diagnosed case of low self-esteem ['If only I could value myself
more! Alas! It is impossible'] bred an exaggerated notion of
how friendly he would need to be in order to have any
friends. And though he was in disagreement with all the
more exalted claims made on friendship's behalf, he was
still deeply concerned with securing affection ['My only
consolation when I am really sad is to love and to be loved'].
Under a heading of 'thoughts that spoil friendship', Proust
confessed to a range of anxieties familiar to any quotidian
emotional paranoiac: 'What did they think of us?' 'Were

we not tactless?' 'Did they like us?' as well as 'The fear of being forgotten in favour of someone else.'

It meant that Proust's overwhelming priority in any encounter was to ensure that he would be liked, remembered and thought well of. 'Not only did he dizzy his hosts and hostesses with verbal compliments, but he ruined himself on flowers and ingenious gifts,' reported his friend Jacques-Émile Blanche, giving a taste of what this priority involved. His psychological insight, so great that it had threatened to put a palm reader out of her job, could be wholly directed towards identifying the appropriate word, smile or flower to win others over. And it worked. He excelled at the art of making friends, he acquired an enormous number, they loved his company, were devoted to him and wrote a pile of adulatory books after his death with titles like *My Friend Marcel Proust* [a volume by Maurice Duplay], *My Friendship with Marcel Proust* [by Fernand Gregh], and *Letters to a Friend* [by Marie Nordlinger].

Given the effort and strategic intelligence he devoted to friendship, it shouldn't surprise us. For instance, it is often assumed, usually by people who don't have many friends, that friendship is a hallowed sphere where what we wish to talk about effortlessly coincides with others' interests. Proust, less optimistic than this, recognized the likelihood of discrepancy, and concluded that he should always be the one to ask questions, and address himself to what was on your mind rather than risk boring you with what was on his.

To do anything else would have been bad conversational manners: 'There is lack of tact in people who in their conversation look not to please others, but to elucidate, egoistically, points that they are interested in.' Conversation required an abdication of oneself in the name of pleasing companions: 'When we chat, it is no longer we who speak . . . we are fashioning ourselves then in the likeness of other people, and not of a self that differs from them.'

It accounts for why Proust's friend Georges de Lauris, a keen rally driver and tennis player, could gratefully report that he had often talked to Proust about sport and motor cars. Of course, Proust cared little for either, but to have insisted on turning the conversation to Mme de Pompadour's childhood with a man keener on Renault's crankshaft would have been to misunderstand what friendship was for.

It was not for elucidating, egotistically, things one was interested in, it was primarily for warmth and affection, which is why, for a cerebral man, Proust had remarkably little interest in overtly intellectual friendships. In the summer of 1920, he received a letter from Sydney Schiff, the friend who would, two years later, engineer his disastrous encounter with Joyce. Sydney told Proust that he was on a seaside holiday in England with his wife Violet, the weather was quite sunny, but Violet had invited a group of hearty young people to stay with them, and he had grown very depressed by how shallow these youngsters were. 'It's very boring for me,' he wrote to Proust, 'because I don't like to be constantly in the company of young people. I am pained by their naivety, which I'm afraid of corrupting, or at least of compromising. Human beings sometimes interest me but I don't like them because they are not intelligent enough.'

Proust, cloistered in bed in Paris, had difficulty appreciating why anyone would be dissatisfied with the idea of spending a holiday on a beach with some young people, whose only fault was not to have read Descartes:

> I do my intellectual work within myself, and once with other people, it's more or less irrelevant to me that they're intelligent, as long as they are *kind*, *sincere*, etc.

When Proust did have intelligent conversations, the priority was still to dedicate himself to others, rather than covertly introduce [as some might] private cerebral concerns. His friend Marcel Plantevignes, the author of yet another volume of reminiscence, this one entitled *With Marcel Proust*, commented on Proust's intellectual courtesy, his concern never to be tiring, hard to follow or categorical in what he said. Proust would frequently punctuate his sentences with a 'perhaps', a 'maybe' or a 'don't you think?'. For Plantevignes, it reflected Proust's desire to please. 'Maybe I'm wrong to tell them what they won't like,' was his underlying thought. Not that Plantevignes was complaining, such tentativeness was welcome, especially on Proust's bad days:

These maybes were very reassuring to encounter in the light of certain rather surprising declarations Proust made on his pessimistic days, and without which they would have made really too much of a shattering impression, thoughts like: 'Friendship doesn't exist,' and 'Love is a trap and only reveals itself to us by making us suffer.'

– Don't you think?

However charming Proust's manners, they might unkindly have been described as overpolite, so much so that the more cynical of Proust's friends invented a mocking term to describe the peculiarities of his social habits. As Fernand Gregh reports:

> We created among ourselves the verb *to proustify* to express a slightly too conscious attitude of geniality, together with what would vulgarly have been called affectations, interminable and delicious.

A representative target of Proust's *proustification* was a middle-aged woman called Laure Haymann, a well-known courtesan, who had once been the mistress of the Duc d'Orléans, the King of Greece, Prince Egon von Fürstenberg and, latterly, Proust's great-uncle, Louis Weil. Proust was in his late teens when he met and first began to *proustify* Laure. He would send her elaborate letters dripping with compliments, accompanied by chocolates, trinkets and flowers, gifts so expensive that his father was forced to lecture him on his extravagance.

'Dear friend, dear delight,' ran a typical note to Laure, accompanied by a little something from the florist, 'Here are fifteen chrysanthemums. I hope the stems will be excessively long, as I requested.' In case they weren't, and in case Laure needed a greater or more enduring token of affection than a collection of long-stemmed plants, he assured Laure that she was a creature of voluptuous intelligence and subtle grace, that she was a divine beauty and a goddess who could turn all men into devoted worshippers. It seemed natural to end the letter by offering affectionate regards and the practical suggestion that: 'I propose to call the present century the century of Laure Haymann.' Laure became his friend.

Here she is, as photographed by Paul Nadar at around the time the chrysanthemums were delivered to her door:

Another favoured target of *proustification* was the poet and novelist Anna de Noailles, responsible for six collections of forgettable poetry, and for Proust a genius worthy of comparison with Baudelaire. When she sent him a copy of her novel *La Domination*, in June 1905, Proust told her that she had given birth to an entire planet, 'a marvellous planet won over for the contemplation of mankind'. Not only was she a cosmic creator, she was also a woman of mythic appearance. 'I have nothing to envy Ulysses because my Athena is more beautiful, has greater genius and knows more than his,' Proust reassured her. A few years later, reviewing a collection of her poetry, *Les Éblouissements*, for *Le Figaro*, he wrote that Anna had created images as sublime as those of Victor Hugo, that her work was a dazzling success and a masterpiece of literary impressionism. To prove the point to his readers, he even quoted a few of Anna's lines:

> *Tandis que détaché d'une invisible fronde,*
> *Un doux oiseau jaillit jusqu'au sommet du monde.*

'Do you know an image more splendid and more perfect than this one?' he asked – at which point his readers could have been forgiven for muttering, well, *yes*, and wondering what had possessed their besotted reviewer.

Was he an extraordinary hypocrite? The word implies that beneath an appearance of good-will and kindness lay a sinister, calculating agenda, and that Proust's real feelings for Laure Haymann and Anna de Noailles could not possibly have matched his extravagant declarations, and were perhaps closer to ridicule than adoration.

The disparity may be less dramatic. No doubt he believed precious few of his proustifications, but he nevertheless remained sincere in the message that had inspired and underlay them: 'I like you and I would like you to like me.' The fifteen long-stemmed chrysanthemums, the marvellous planets, the devoted worshippers, the Athenas, goddesses and splendid images were merely what Proust felt he would need to add to his own presence in order to secure affection, in the light of his previously mentioned debilitating assessment of his own qualities ['I certainly think less of myself than Antoine (his butler) does of himself'].

In fact, the exaggerated scale of Proust's social politeness should not blind us to the degree of insincerity every friendship demands, the ever-present requirement to deliver an affable but hollow word to a friend who proudly shows us a volume of their poetry or newborn baby. To call such politeness hypocrisy is to neglect that we have lied in a local way not in order to conceal fundamentally malevolent intentions but rather to confirm our sense of affection, which might have been doubted if there had been no gasping and praising, because of the unusual intensity of people's attachment to their verse and children. There seems a gap between what others need to hear from us in order to trust that we like them, and the extent of the negative thoughts we know we can feel towards them and *still* like them. We know it is possible to think of someone as both dismal at poetry and perceptive, both inclined to pomposity and charming, both suffering from halitosis and genial. But the susceptibility of others means that the negative part of the equation can rarely be expressed without jeopardizing the union. We usually believe gossip about ourselves to have been inspired by a level of malice far greater [or more critical] than the malice we ourselves felt in relation to the last person we gossiped about, a person whose habits we could mock without this in any way altering our affection for them.

Proust once compared friendship to reading, because both activities involved communion with others, but added that reading had a key advantage:

> In reading, friendship is suddenly brought back to its original purity. There is no false amiability with books. If we spend the evening with these friends, it is because we genuinely want to.

Whereas in life we are often led to have dinner because we fear for the future of a valued friendship were we to decline the invitation, a hypocritical meal forced upon us by an awareness of our friend's unwarranted yet unavoidable susceptibility. How much more honest we can be with books. There at least we can turn to them when we want, and look bored or cut short a dialogue as soon as necessary.

Had we been granted the opportunity to spend an evening with Molière, even this comic genius would have forced us into an occasional fake smile, which is why Proust expressed a preference for communion with the page-bound rather than the living playwright. At least, in book form:

> We laugh at what Molière has to say only in so far as we find it funny; when he bores us, we are not afraid to look bored, and once we have definitely had enough of him, we put him back in his place as abruptly as if he had neither genius nor celebrity.

How are we to respond to the level of insincerity apparently required in every friendship? How are we to respond to the two habitually conflicting projects carried on under the single umbrella of friendship, a project to secure affection, and a project to express ourselves honestly? It was because Proust was both unusually honest and unusually affectionate that he drove the joint project to breaking point and came up with his distinctive approach to friendship, which was to judge that the pursuit of affection and the pursuit of truth were fundamentally rather than occasionally incompatible. It meant adopting a much narrower conception of what friendship was for: it was for playful exchanges with Laure, but not for telling Molière that he was boring and Anna de Noailles that she couldn't write poetry. One might imagine that it made Proust a far lesser friend, but paradoxically the radical separation had the power to make him both a better, more loyal, more charming friend, *and* a more honest, profound and unsentimental thinker.

An example of how this separation influenced Proust's behaviour can be seen in his friendship with Fernand Gregh, a one-time classmate and fellow writer. When Proust published his first collection of stories, Fernand Gregh was in an influential position on the literary paper, *La Revue de Paris*. Despite the many flaws of *Pleasures and Regrets*, it was not too much to hope that an old schoolfriend could put in a nice word for the book, but it did prove too much to hope of Gregh, who failed even to mention Proust's writing to the readers of *La Revue de Paris*. He found space for a little review, but there talked only of the illustrations, the preface and the piano pieces which had come with the book and which Proust had had nothing to do with, and then added sarcastic jibes about the connections Proust had used in order to get his work published.

What do you do when a friend like Gregh subsequently writes a book of his own, a very bad one at that, and sends a copy asking for your opinion? Proust faced the question only a few weeks later, when Fernand sent him *The House of Childhood*, a collection of poems in the light of which Anna de Noailles's work could truly have been compared to Baudelaire's. Proust might have taken this opportunity to confront Gregh on his behaviour, told him the truth about his poetry and suggested he hold on to his day job. But we know this wasn't Proust's style, and we find him writing a generous letter of congratulation. 'What I have read struck me as really *beautiful*,' Proust told Fernand. 'I know you were hard on my book. But that no doubt was because you thought it bad. For the same reason, finding yours good, I am glad to tell you so and to tell others.'

More interesting than the letters we send our friends may be the ones we finish, then decide not to post after all. Found among his papers after his death was a note Proust had written to Gregh a little before the one he actually sent. It contained a far nastier, far less acceptable, but far truer message. It thanked Gregh for *The House of Childhood*, but then limited itself to praising the quantity rather than the quality of this poetic output, and went on to make wounding reference to Gregh's pride, distrustfulness and childlike soul.

Why didn't he send it? Though the dominant view of grievances is that they should invariably be discussed with their progenitors, the typically unsatisfactory results of doing so should perhaps urge us to reconsider. Proust might have invited Gregh to a restaurant, offered him the finest grapes on a vine plant, pressed a five-hundred-franc tip into the waiter's hand for good measure, and begun to tell his friend in the gentlest voice that he seemed a little too proud, had some problems with trust and that his soul was a touch childlike; only to find Gregh turning red, pushing aside the grapes and walking angrily out of the restaurant, to the surprise of the richly remunerated waiter. What would this have achieved, aside from unnecessarily alienating proud Gregh? And anyway, had Proust really become friends with this character in order to share his palm reader's insights with him?

Instead, these awkward thoughts were better entertained elsewhere, in a private space designed for analyses too wounding to be shared with those who had inspired them. A letter which never gets sent is such a place. A novel is another.

One way of considering *In Search of Lost Time* is as an unusually long unsent letter, the antidote to a lifetime of proustification, the flipside of the Athenas, lavish gifts and long-stemmed chrysanthemums, the place where the unsayable was finally granted expression. Having described artists as 'creatures who talk of precisely the things one shouldn't mention', the novel gave Proust the chance to mention them all. Laure Haymann might have had her ravishing sides, but she also had less worthy ones, and these migrated into the representation of the fictional Odette de Crécy. Fernand Gregh might have avoided a lecture from Proust in real life, but he received a covert one in Proust's damning portrait of Alfred Bloch, for whom he was in part the model.

Unfortunately for Proust, the attempt to be honest *and* keep his friends was somewhat marred by the vulgar insistence of members of Parisian society to read his work as a *roman-à-clef*. 'There are no keys to the characters of this book,' insisted Proust, but even so, the keys took grave offence, among them Camille Barrère for finding bits of himself in Norpois, Robert de Montesquiou for finding bits of himself in the Baron de Charlus, the Duc d'Albufera for recognizing his love affair with Louisa de Mornand in Robert de Saint-Loup's affair with Rachel, and Laure for finding traits of herself in Odette de Crécy. Though Proust rushed to assure Laure that in fact Odette was 'exactly the opposite of you', it wasn't surprising that she had difficulty believing him, given that even their addresses were the same. The Paris Yellow Pages of Proust's time refers to: 'HAYMANN (Mme Laure), rue Lapérouse, 3', and the novel to Odette's 'little hotel, on the rue La Pérouse, behind the Arc de Triomphe'. The only ambiguity seems to be the spelling of the street.

Despite these hiccups, the principle of separating what belongs to friendship and what belongs to the unsent letter or novel can still be defended [albeit with a proviso that one changes the street names and keeps the letters well hidden].

It may even be defended in the name of friendship. Proust proposed that 'the scorners of friendship can ... be the finest friends in the world', perhaps because these scorners approach the bond with more realistic expectations. They avoid talking at length about themselves, not because they think the subject unimportant, but rather because they recognize it as too important to be placed at the mercy of the haphazard, fleeting and ultimately superficial medium that is conversation. It means they have no resentment about asking rather than answering questions, seeing friendship as a domain in which to learn about, not lecture others. Furthermore, because they appreciate others' susceptibilities, they accept a resultant need for a degree of false amiability, for a rose-tinted interpretation of an ageing ex-courtesan's appearance or for a generous review of a well-intentioned but pedestrian volume of poetry.

Rather than militantly pursue both truth and affection, they discern the incompatibilities, and so divide their projects, making a wise separation between the chrysanthemums and the novel, between Laure Haymann and Odette de Crécy, between the letter which gets sent and the one that stays hidden but nevertheless needs to be written.

CHAPTER SEVEN

HOW TO OPEN
YOUR EYES

Proust once wrote an essay in which he set out to restore a smile to the face of a gloomy, envious and dissatisfied young man. He pictured this young man sitting at table after lunch one day in his parents' flat, gazing dejectedly at his surroundings: at a knife left lying on the tablecloth, at the remains of an underdone, tasteless cutlet and a half turned-back tablecloth. He would see his mother at the far end of the dining room doing her knitting, and the family cat curled up on top of a cupboard next to a bottle of brandy being kept for a special occasion. The mundanity of the scene would contrast with the young man's taste for beautiful and costly things, which he lacked the money to acquire. Proust imagined the revulsion the young aesthete would feel at this bourgeois interior, and how he would compare it to the splendours he had seen in museums and cathedrals. He would envy those bankers who had enough money to decorate their houses properly, so that everything in them was beautiful, was a work of art, right down to the coal tongs in the fireplace and the knobs on the doors.

To escape his domestic gloom, if he couldn't catch the next train to Holland or Italy, the young man might leave the flat and go to the Louvre, where at least he could feast his eyes on splendid things: grand palaces painted by Veronese, harbour scenes by Claude and princely lives by Van Dyck.

Touched by his predicament, Proust proposed to make a radical change to the young man's life by way of a modest alteration to his museum itinerary. Rather than let him hurry to galleries hung with paintings by Claude and Veronese, Proust suggested leading him to a quite different part of the museum, to those galleries hung with the works of Jean-Baptiste Chardin.

It might have seemed an odd choice, for Chardin hadn't painted many harbours, princes or palaces. He liked to depict bowls of fruit, jugs, coffee pots, loaves of bread, knives, glasses of wine and slabs of meat. He liked painting kitchen utensils, not just pretty chocolate jars, but salt cellars and strainers. When it came to people, Chardin's figures were rarely doing anything heroic; one was reading a book, another was building a house of cards, a woman had just come home from the market with a couple of loaves of bread and a mother was showing her daughter some mistakes she had made in her needlework.

Yet, in spite of the ordinary nature of their subjects, Chardin's paintings succeeded in being extraordinarily beguiling and evocative. A peach by him was as pink and chubby as a cherub, a plate of oysters or a slice of lemon were tempting symbols of gluttony and sensuality. A skate, slit open and hanging from a hook, evoked the sea of which it had been a fearsome denizen in its lifetime. Its insides, coloured with a deep red blood, blue nerves and white muscles, were like the naves of a polychrome cathedral.

There was a harmony too between objects; in one canvas, almost a friendship between the reddish colours of a hearthrug, a needle box and a skein of wool. These paintings were windows on to a world at once recognizably our own, yet uncommonly, wonderfully tempting.

After an encounter with Chardin, Proust had high hopes for the spiritual transformation of his sad young man.

> Once he had been dazzled by this opulent depiction of what he called mediocrity, this appetizing depiction of a life he had found insipid, this great art of nature he had thought paltry, I should say to him: 'Are you happy?'

Why would he be? Because Chardin had shown him that the kind of environment in which he lived could, for a fraction of the cost, have many of the charms he had previously associated only with palaces and the princely life. No longer would he feel painfully excluded from an aesthetic realm, no longer would he be so envious of smart bankers with gold-plated coal tongs and diamond-studded door handles. He would learn that metal and earthenware could also be enchanting, and common crockery as beautiful as precious stones. After looking at Chardin's work, even the humblest rooms in his parents' flat would have the power to delight him, Proust promised:

> When you walk around a kitchen, you will say to yourself, this is interesting, this is grand, this is beautiful like a Chardin.

Having started on his essay, Proust tried to interest Pierre Mainguet, the editor of the arts magazine the *Revue Hebdomadaire*, in its contents.

> I have just written a little study in the philosophy of art, if I may use that slightly pretentious phrase, in which I have tried to show how the great painters initiate us into a knowledge and love of the external world, how they are the ones 'by whom our eyes are opened', opened, that is, on the world. In this study, I use the work of Chardin as an example, and I try to show its influence on our life, the charm and wisdom with which it coats our most modest moments by initiating us into the *life* of still life. Do you think this sort of study would interest the readers of the *Revue Hebdomadaire*?

Perhaps, but since its editor was sure it wouldn't, they had no chance to find out. Turning the piece down was an understandable oversight: this was 1895, and Mainguet didn't know Proust would one day be *Proust*. What is more, the moral of the essay lay not too far from the ridiculous. It was only a step away from suggesting that everything down to the last lemon was beautiful, that there was no good reason to be envious of any condition beside our own, that a hovel was as nice as a villa and an emerald no better than a chipped plate.

However, instead of urging us to place the *same* value on all things, Proust might more interestingly have been encouraging us to ascribe them their *correct* value, and hence to revise certain notions of the good life, which risked inspiring an unfair neglect of some settings and a misguided enthusiasm for others. If it hadn't been for Pierre Mainguet's rejection, the readers of the *Revue Hebdomadaire* would have benefited from a chance to reappraise their conceptions of beauty, and could have entered into a new and possibly more rewarding relationship with salt cellars, crockery and apples.

Why would they previously have lacked such a relationship? Why wouldn't they have appreciated their tableware and fruit? At one level, such questions seem superfluous; it just appears *natural* to be struck by the beauty of some things and to be left cold by others, there is no conscious rumination or decision behind our choice of what appeals to us visually, we simply know we are moved by palaces but not by kitchens, by porcelain but not by china, by guavas but not apples.

However, the immediacy with which aesthetic judgements arise should not fool us into assuming that their origins are entirely natural or their verdicts unalterable. Proust's letter to Monsieur Mainguet hinted as much. By saying that great painters were the ones by whom our eyes were opened, Proust was at the same time implying that our sense of beauty was not immobile, and could be sensitized by painters who would, through their canvases, educate us into an appreciation of once neglected aesthetic qualities. If the dissatisfied young man had failed to consider the family tableware or fruit, it was in part out of a lack of acquaintance with images which would have shown him the key to their attractions.

Great painters possess such power to open our eyes because of the unusual receptivity of their own eyes to aspects of visual experience; to the play of light on the end of a spoon, the fibrous softness of a tablecloth, the velvety skin of a peach or the pinkish tones of an old man's skin. We might caricature the history of art as a succession of geniuses engaged in pointing out different elements worthy of our attention, a succession of painters using their immense technical mastery to say what amounts to, 'Aren't those back streets in Delft pretty?' or, 'Isn't the Seine nice outside Paris?' And in Chardin's case, to say to the world, and some of the dissatisfied young men within it, 'Look not just at the Roman campagna, the pageantry of Venice and the proud expression of Charles I astride his horse, but also, have a look at the bowl on the sideboard, the dead fish in your kitchen and the crusty bread loaves in the hall.'

The happiness which may emerge from taking a second look is central to Proust's therapeutic conception, it reveals the extent to which our dissatisfactions may be the result of failing to look properly at our lives rather than the result of anything inherently deficient about them. Appreciating the beauty of crusty loaves does not preclude our interest in a château, but failing to do so must call into question our overall capacity for appreciation. The gap between what the dissatisfied youth could see in his flat and what Chardin noticed in very similar interiors places the emphasis on a certain way of looking, as opposed to a mere process of acquiring or possessing.

The young man in the Chardin essay of 1895 was not the last Proustian character to be unhappy because he couldn't open his eyes. He shared important similarities with another dissatisfied Proustian hero, who appeared some eighteen years later. The Chardin youth and the narrator of *In Search of Lost Time* were both suffering from depression and were both living in a world drained of interest when they were both rescued by a vision of their world which presented it in its true yet unexpectedly glorious colours, and which reminded them of their failure to open their eyes adequately until then – the only difference being that one of these glorious visions came from a gallery in the Louvre, and the other from a boulangerie.

To outline the baking case, Proust describes his narrator sitting at home one winter's afternoon, suffering from a cold, and feeling rather dispirited by the dreary day he has had, with only the prospect of another dreary day ahead of him tomorrow. His mother comes into the room and asks if he'd like a cup of lime-blossom tea. He declines her offer, but then, for no particular reason, changes his mind. To accompany this tea, his mother brings him a madeleine, a squat, plump little cake which looks as if it had been moulded in the fluted valve of a scallop shell. The dispirited, rheumatic narrator breaks off a morsel, drops it into the tea and takes a sip, at which point something miraculous happens:

> No sooner had the warm liquid mixed with the crumbs touched my palate than a shiver ran through me and I stopped, intent upon the extraordinary thing that was happening to me. An exquisite pleasure had invaded my senses, something isolated, detached, with no suggestion of its origin. And at once the vicissitudes of life had become indifferent to me, its disaster innocuous, its brevity illusory ... I had ceased now to feel mediocre, contingent, mortal.

What sort of madeleine was this? None other than the kind which aunt Léonie used to dip into her tea and give to the narrator's childhood self, on Sundays when he would come into her bedroom and say good morning to her, during the holidays his family used to spend at her house in the country town of Combray. Like much of his life, the narrator's childhood has grown rather vague in his mind since then, and what he does remember of it holds no particular charm or interest. It doesn't mean it actually lacked charm, it might just be that he has forgotten what happened – and it is this failure which the madeleine now addresses. By a quirk of physiology, a cake which has not crossed his lips since childhood and therefore remains uncorrupted by later associations has the ability to carry him back to Combray days, introducing him to a stream of rich and intimate memories of the past. Childhood at once seems a more beautiful period than he had remembered, he recalls with new-found wonder the old grey house in which aunt Léonie used to live, the town and surroundings of Combray, the streets along which he used to run errands, the parish church, the country roads, the flowers in Léonie's garden and the water lilies floating on the Vivone river. And in so doing he recognizes the worth of these memories, which inspire the novel he will eventually narrate, which is in a sense an entire, extended, controlled 'Proustian moment', to which it is akin in sensitivity and sensual immediacy.

If the incident with the madeleine cheers the narrator, it is because it helps him realize that it isn't his *life* which has been mediocre so much as the *image* of it he possessed in memory. It is a key Proustian distinction, as therapeutically relevant in his case as it was for the Chardin young man:

> The reason why life may be judged to be trivial although at certain moments it seems to us so beautiful is that we form our judgement, ordinarily, not on the evidence of life itself but of those quite different images which preserve nothing of life – and therefore we judge it disparagingly.

These poor images arise out of our failure to register a scene properly at the time, and hence to remember anything of its reality thereafter. Indeed, Proust suggests that we have a better chance of generating vivid images of our past when we are involuntarily jogged into remembering it by a madeleine, a long-forgotten smell or an old glove, than when we voluntarily and intellectually attempt to evoke it:

> Voluntary memory, the memory of the intellect and the eyes, [gives] us only imprecise facsimiles of the past which no more resemble it than pictures by bad painters resemble the spring ... So we don't believe that life is beautiful because we don't *recall* it, but if we get a whiff of a long-forgotten smell we are suddenly intoxicated, and similarly we *think* we no longer love the dead, because we don't remember them, but if by chance we come across an old glove we burst into tears.

A few years before he died, Proust received a questionnaire asking him to list his eight favourite French paintings in the Louvre [into which he hadn't stepped for fifteen years].

His wavering answer: Watteau's *L'Embarquement* or perhaps *L'Indifférent*; three paintings by Chardin, a self-portrait, a portrait of his wife, and *Nature Morte*; Manet's *Olympia*; a Renoir, or perhaps Corot's *La Barque du Dante*, or maybe his *La Cathédrale de Chartres*; and finally, Millet's *Le Printemps*.

So we have an idea of a good Proustian painting of spring, which he would presumably have judged to be as capable of evoking the actual qualities of spring as involuntary memory was of evoking the actual qualities of the past. But what does a good painter put into his canvases which an indifferent one leaves out, which is another way of asking what separates voluntary from involuntary memory? One answer is 'not very much', or at least, surprisingly little. It is remarkable to what extent bad paintings of spring resemble, though are still distinct from, good ones. Bad painters may be excellent draughtsmen, good on clouds, clever on budding leaves, dutiful on roots, and yet still lack a command of those elusive elements in which the particular charms of spring are lodged. They cannot, for instance, depict, and hence make us notice, the pinkish border on the edge of the blossom of a tree, the contrast between storm and sunshine in the light across a field, the gnarled quality of bark or the vulnerable, tentative appearance of flowers on the side of a country track — small details, no doubt, but in the end, the only things on which our sense of, and enthusiasm for springtime can be based.

Similarly, what separates involuntary from voluntary memory is both infinitesimal and critical. Before he tasted the legendary tea and madeleine, the narrator was not devoid of memories of his childhood, it wasn't as though he had forgotten where in France he went on holiday as a child [Combray or Clermont-Ferrand?], what the river was called [Vivone or Varone?] and with which relative he had stayed [aunt Léonie or Lily?]. Yet these memories were lifeless because they lacked the equivalent of the touches of the good painter, the awareness of light falling across Combray's central square in mid-afternoon, the smell of aunt Léonie's bedroom, the moistness of the air on the banks of the Vivone, the sound of the garden bell and the aroma of fresh asparagus for lunch, details which suggest it would be more accurate to describe the madeleine as provoking a moment of *appreciation* rather than mere *recollection*.

Why don't we appreciate things more widely? The problem goes beyond inattention or laziness. It may also stem from insufficient exposure to images of beauty, which are close enough to our own world in order to guide and inspire us. The young man in Proust's essay was dissatisfied because he only knew Veronese, Claude and Van Dyck, who did not depict worlds akin to his own, and his knowledge of art history failed to include Chardin, who he so badly needed to point out the interest of his kitchen. The omission seems representative. Whatever the efforts of certain great artists to open our eyes to our world, they cannot prevent us from being surrounded by numerous less helpful images which, with no sinister intentions and often with great artistry, nevertheless have the effect of suggesting to us that there is a depressing gap between our own life and the realm of beauty.

As a boy, Proust's narrator develops a desire to go to the seaside. He imagines how beautiful it must be to go to Normandy, and in particular to a resort he has heard of called Balbec. However, he is under the thrall of some hazardously antiquated images of seaside life, which appear to have come out of a book on the medieval Gothic period. He pictures a coastline shrouded in great banks of mist and fog, pounded by a furious sea, he pictures isolated churches that are as rugged and precipitous as cliffs, with their towers echoing to the sound of wailing seabirds and

deafening wind. As for the locals, he imagines a Normandy inhabited by the descendants of the proud ancient mythical tribe of the Cimmerians, a people described by Homer as living in a mysterious land of perpetual darkness.

Such an image of seaside beauty explains the narrator's travel difficulties, for when he gets to Balbec, he finds a typical early-twentieth-century beach resort. The place is full of restaurants, shops, motor cars and cyclists, there are people going swimming and walking along the seafront with their parasols, there is a grand hotel, with a luxurious lobby, a lift, bellboys and a huge dining room whose plate-glass window looks out on to a completely calm sea, bathed in glorious sunshine.

Except that none of this is glorious to the medieval Gothic narrator, who had been so looking forward to those precipitous cliffs, those wailing seabirds and that howling wind.

The disappointment illustrates the critical importance of images in our appreciation of our surroundings, together with the risks of leaving home with the wrong ones. A picture of cliffs and seabirds wailing may be enchanting, but it will lead to problems when it is six hundred years out of line with the reality of our holiday destination.

Though the narrator experiences a particularly extreme gap between his surroundings and his internal conception of beauty, it is arguable that a degree of discrepancy is characteristic of modern life. Because of the speed of technological and architectural change, the world is liable to be full of scenes and objects which have not yet been transformed into appropriate images, and may therefore make us nostalgic for another, now lost world, which is not inherently more beautiful, but might seem it because it has already been so widely depicted by those who open our eyes. There is a danger of developing a blanket distaste for modern life, which could have its attractions but lack the all-important images to help us identify them.

Fortunately for the narrator and his holiday, the painter Elstir has also come to Balbec, ready to create his own images rather than rely on those from old books. He has been at work painting local scenes: pictures of women in cotton dresses, of yachts out at sea, of harbours, seascapes and a nearby racecourse. Furthermore, he invites the narrator to his studio. Standing in front of a painting of a racecourse, the narrator shyly admits that he's never been tempted to go there, which isn't surprising, given that his interests lie solely in stormy seas and wailing seabirds. However, Elstir suggests that he has been hasty and helps him to take a second look. He draws his attention to one of the jockeys, sitting in a paddock, gloomy and grey faced in a bright jacket, reining in a rearing horse, then points out how elegant women look at race meetings when they arrive in their carriages, and stand with their binoculars, bathed in a particular kind of sunlight, almost Dutch in tone, in which you can feel the coldness of the water.

The narrator has been avoiding not only racecourses, but also the seashore. He has been looking at the sea with his fingers in front of his eyes, in order to blot out any modern ships that might pass by and spoil his attempt to view the sea in an immemorial state, or at least as it must have looked no later than the early centuries of Greece. Again, Elstir rescues him from his peculiar habit, and draws his attention to the beauty of yachts. He points out their uniform surfaces, which are simple, gleaming and grey and which, in the bluish haze reflecting off the sea, take on a seductive creamy softness. He talks of the women on board, who dress attractively in white cotton or linen clothes, which in the sunlight, against the blue of the sea, take on the dazzling whiteness of a spread sail.

After this encounter with Elstir and his canvases, the narrator has a chance to update his images of seaside beauty by a vital few centuries, and thereby saves his holiday.

> I realized that regattas and race meetings where well-dressed women could be seen bathed in the greenish light of a marine racecourse, might be as interesting for a modern artist as those festivities that Veronese and Carpaccio loved to depict.

The incident emphasizes once more that beauty is something to be found, rather than passively encountered, that it requires us to pick up on certain details, to identify the whiteness of a cotton dress, the reflection of the sea on the hull of a yacht or the contrast between the colour of a jockey's coat and his face. It also emphasizes how vulnerable we are to depression when the Elstirs of the world choose not to go on holiday and the pre-prepared images run out, when our knowledge of art does not stretch any later than Carpaccio [1450–1525] and Veronese [1528–1588] and we see a two-hundred-horsepower Sunseeker accelerating out of the marina. It may genuinely be an unattractive example of aquatic transport; then again, our objection to the speedboat may stem from nothing other than a stubborn adherence to ancient images of beauty, and a resistance to a process of active appreciation which even Veronese and Carpaccio would have undertaken had they been in our place.

*

The images with which we are surrounded are often not just out of date, they can also be unhelpfully ostentatious. When Proust urges us to evaluate the world properly, he repeatedly reminds us of the value of modest scenes. Chardin opens our eyes to the beauty of salt cellars and jugs, the madeleine delights the narrator by evoking memories of an ordinary bourgeois childhood, Elstir paints nothing grander than cotton dresses and harbours. In Proust's view, such modesty is characteristic of beauty:

> True beauty is indeed the one thing incapable of answering the expectations of an over-romantic imagination . . . What disappointments has it not caused since it first appeared to the mass of mankind! A woman goes to see a masterpiece of art as excitedly as if she was finishing a serial-story, or consulting a fortune teller or waiting for her lover. But she sees a man sitting meditating by the window, in a room where there is not much light. She waits for a moment in case something more may appear, as in a boulevard transparency. And though hypocrisy may seal her lips, she says in her heart of hearts: 'What, is that all there is to Rembrandt's *Philosopher*?'

A philosopher whose interest is of course understated, subtle, calm . . . It all amounts to an intimate, democratic, unsnobbish vision of beauty, one safely in reach of a bourgeois salary and devoid of anything imposing or aristocratic.

However touching, this does sit somewhat uneasily with

evidence that Proust himself had rather a taste for ostentation, and frequently behaved in ways diametrically opposed to the spirit of Chardin or Rembrandt's *Philosopher*. The accusations run something like this.

— *That he had elaborate names in his address book*

Though he grew up in a bourgeois family, Proust acquired as friends a more than coincidental range of aristocratic figures with names like the Duc de Clermont-Tonnerre, the Comte Gabriel de la Rochefoucauld, the Comte Robert de Montesquiou-Fezensac, the Prince Edmond de Polignac, the Comte Philibert de Salignac-Fénelon, the Prince Constantin de Brancovan and the Princesse Alexandre de Caraman-Chimay.

— *That he went to the Ritz all the time*

Though he was well catered for at home, and had a maid adept at preparing wholesome meals, and a dining room in which to give dinner parties, Proust repeatedly ate out and entertained at the Ritz in the Place Vendôme, where he would order sumptuous meals for friends, add a two hundred per cent service charge to the bill and drink champagne from fluted glasses.

— *That he went to many parties*

In fact, so many that André Gide first turned down his novel at Gallimard for the well-founded literary reason that he believed this to be the work of a manic socialite. As he later explained, 'For me, you had remained the man who frequented the house of Madame X, Y, Z, the man who wrote for the *Figaro*. I thought of you as – shall I confess it? – . . . a snob, a dilettante, a socialite.'

Proust was ready with an honest answer. It was true he had been attracted to the ostentatious life, he had sought to frequent the house of Madame X, Y and Z and had tried to befriend any aristocrats who happened to be there [aristocrats whose extraordinary glamour in Proust's day should be compared to the subsequent glamour of film stars, lest it be too easy to acquire a self-righteous sense of virtue on the basis of never having taken an interest in dukes].

However, the end of the story is important, namely, that Proust was disappointed by glamour when he found it. He went to Mme Y's parties, sent flowers to Mme Z, ingratiated himself with the Prince Constantin de Brancovan, and then realized he had been sold a lie. The images of glamour which had instilled the desire to pursue aristocrats simply did not match the realities of aristocratic life. He recognized that he was better off staying at home, that he could be as happy talking to his maid as to the Princesse Caraman-Chimay.

Proust's narrator experiences a similar trajectory of hope and disappointment. He begins by being drawn to the aura of the Duc and Duchesse de Guermantes, picturing them as belonging to a superior race infused with the poetry of their ancient name, dating back to the earliest, noblest families of France, and a time so distant that not even the cathedrals of Paris and Chartres were yet built. He imagines the Guermantes wrapped in the mystery of the Merovingian age, they make him think of forest hunting scenes in medieval tapestries and seem to be made of a different substance from humans, existing like figures in a stained-glass window. He dreams of how exquisite it would be to spend the day with the Duchesse fishing for trout in her sumptuous ducal park, filled with flowers, rivulets and fountains.

Then he has a chance to meet the Guermantes, and the image shatters. Far from being made of a different substance from other humans, the Guermantes are much like anyone else, only with less developed tastes and opinions. The Duc is a coarse, cruel, vulgar man, his wife is keener to be sharp and witty than sincere, and the guests at their table, who he had previously imagined like the Apostles in the Sainte-Chapelle, are concerned only to gossip and exchange trivialities.

Such disastrous encounters with aristocrats might encourage us to give up on our search for so-called eminent figures, who only turn out to be vulgar drones when we meet them. The snobbish longing to associate with those of superior rank should, it seems, be abandoned in favour of a gracious accommodation to our lot.

Yet there may be a different conclusion to be drawn. Rather than ceasing to discriminate between people altogether, we may simply have to become better at doing so. The image of a refined aristocracy is not false, it is merely dangerously uncomplicated. There are of course superior people at large in the world, but it is optimistic to assume that they could be so conveniently located on the basis of their surname. It is this the snob refuses to believe, trusting instead in the existence of watertight classes whose members unfailingly display certain qualities. Though a few aristocrats can match expectations, a great many more will have the winning qualities of the Duc de Guermantes, for the category of 'aristocracy' is simply too crude a net to pick up on something as unpredictably allocated as virtue or refinement. There may be someone worthy of the expectations which the narrator has harboured of the Duc de Guermantes, but this person might well appear in the unexpected guise of an electrician, cook or lawyer.

It is this unexpectedness which Proust eventually recognized. Late in life, when a certain Mme Sert wrote and bluntly asked him whether he was a snob, he replied:

> If, amongst the very rare friends who out of habit continue to come and ask for news of me, there still passes now and then a duke or a prince, they are largely made up for by other friends, one of whom is a valet and the other a driver . . . It's hard to choose between them. Valets are more educated than dukes, and speak a nicer French, but they are more fastidious about etiquette and less simple, more susceptible. At the end of the day, one can't choose between them. The driver has more class.

The scenario may have been exaggerated for Mme Sert, but the moral was clear; that qualities like education or an ability to express oneself well did not follow simple paths, and that one could not therefore evaluate people on the basis of conspicuous categories. Just as Chardin had illustrated to the sad young man that beauty did not always lie in obvious places, so too the valet who spoke lovely French served to remind Proust [or perhaps just Mme Sert] that refinement was not conveniently tethered to its image.

Simple images are nevertheless attractive in their lack of ambiguity. Before he saw Chardin's paintings, the sad young man could at least believe that all bourgeois interiors were inferior to palaces, and could therefore make a simple equation between palaces and happiness. Before meeting aristocrats, Proust could at least trust in the existence of an entire class of superior beings, and could equate meeting them with acquiring a fulfilled social life. How much more difficult to factor in sumptuous bourgeois kitchens, boring princes and drivers with more class than dukes. Simple images provide certainties; for instance, they assure us that financial expenditure is a guarantor of enjoyment:

> One sees people who are doubtful whether the sight of the sea and the sound of its waves are really enjoyable, but who become convinced that they are – and also convinced of the rare quality of their wholly detached tastes – when they have agreed to pay a hundred francs a day for a room in a hotel which will enable them to enjoy this sight and sound.

Similarly, there are people who are doubtful whether or not someone is intelligent, but who rapidly become convinced that they are once they see them fit the dominant image of an intelligent person, and learn of their formal education, factual knowledge and university degree.

Such people would have had no difficulty in recognizing that Proust's maid was an idiot: she thought that Napoleon and Bonaparte were two different people, and refused to believe Proust for a week when he suggested otherwise. But Proust knew she was brilliant ['I've never managed to teach her to spell, and she has never had the patience to read even half a page of my book, but she is full of extraordinary gifts']. This isn't to propose an equally, if more perversely, snobbish argument that education has no value, and that the importance of European history from Campo Formio to the Battle of Waterloo is the result of a sinister academic conspiracy, but rather that an ability to identify emperors and spell aproximately is not in itself enough to establish the existence of something as hard to define as intelligence.

Albertine has never been on a history of art course. One summer afternoon in Proust's novel she is sitting on a hotel terrace in Balbec, talking to Mme de Cambremer, her daughter-in-law, a barrister friend of theirs and the narrator. Suddenly, out at sea, a group of gulls which have been floating on top of the water take off noisily.

'I love them; I saw them in Amsterdam,' says Albertine. 'They smell of the sea, they come and sniff the salt air even through the paving stones.'

'Ah, so you've been to Holland. Do you know the

Vermeers?' asks Mme de Cambremer. Albertine replies that unfortunately she doesn't know them, at which point Proust quietly shares with us Albertine's even more unfortunate belief that these Vermeers are a group of Dutch people, not canvases in the Rijksmuseum.

Luckily, the lacuna in her knowledge of art history goes by undetected, though one can imagine Mme de Cambremer's horror had she discovered it. Nervous of her own ability to respond correctly to art, the external signs of artistic awareness take on a disproportionate significance for an art snob, like Mme de Cambremer. Much as for the social snob, unable to judge others independently, a title or reputation becomes the only guide to eminence, so too for the art snob information is ferociously clung to as a marker of artistic appreciation – though Albertine would only need to make another, more culturally aware trip to Amsterdam in order to discover what she had missed. She might even appreciate Vermeer far more than Mme de Cambremer, for in her naivety there would at least be a potential for sincerity absent from de Cambremer's exaggerated respect for art, which ironically ends up treating canvases far more like a family of Dutch burghers whom one would be privileged to meet.

The moral? That we shouldn't deny the bread on the sideboard a place in our conception of beauty, that we should shoot the painter rather than the spring, and blame memory rather than what is remembered; that we should restrain our expectations when introduced to a Comte de Salignac-Fénelon-de-Clermont-Tonnerre, and avoid fixating on spelling mistakes and alternative histories of Imperial France when meeting those less elaborately titled.

CHAPTER EIGHT

How to Be Happy in Love

Q: Would Proust really be someone to consult for advice on romantic problems?
A: Perhaps – in spite of the evidence. He outlined his credentials in a letter to André Gide.

> Incapable though I am of obtaining anything for myself, of sparing myself the least ill, I have been endowed (and it's certainly my only gift) with the power to procure, very often, the happiness of others, to relieve them from pain. I have reconciled not only enemies, but lovers, I've cured invalids while being capable only of worsening my own illness, I've made idlers work while remaining idle myself ... The qualities (I tell you this quite unaffectedly because in other respects I have a very poor opinion of myself) which give me these chances of success on behalf of other people are, together with a certain diplomacy, a capacity for self-forgetfulness and an exclusive concentration on my friends' welfare, qualities which are not often met with in the same person ... I felt while I was writing my book that if Swann had known me and had been able to make use of me, I should have known how to bring Odette round to him.

Q: Swann and Odette?
A: One shouldn't necessarily equate the misfortunes of individual fictional characters with the author's overall prognosis for human contentment. Trapped inside a novel,

these unhappy characters would, after all, be the only ones unable to draw the therapeutic benefits of reading it.

Q: Did he think that love could last for ever?
A: Well, no, but the limits to eternity didn't lie specifically with love. They lay in the general difficulty of maintaining an appreciative relationship with anything or anyone that was always around.

Q: What kind of difficulties?
A: Take the unemotive example of the telephone. Bell invented it in 1876. By 1900, there were thirty thousand phones in France. Proust rapidly acquired one [tel. 29205] and particularly liked a service called the 'theatre-phone', which allowed him to listen live to opera and theatre in Paris venues.

He might have appreciated his phone, but he noted how quickly everyone else began taking theirs for granted. As early as 1907, he wrote that the machine was

> a supernatural instrument before whose miracle we used to stand amazed, and which we now employ without giving it a thought, to summon our tailor or to order an ice cream.

Moreover, if the confiserie had a busy line or the connection to the tailor a hum, instead of admiring the technological advances which had frustrated our sophisticated desires, there was a tendency to react with childish ingratitude:

Since we are children who play with divine forces without shuddering before their mystery, we only find the telephone 'convenient', or rather, as we are spoilt children, we find that 'it isn't convenient', we fill *Le Figaro* with our complaints.

A mere thirty-one years separated Bell's invention from Proust's sad observations on the state of French telephone-appreciation. It had taken a little more than three decades for a technological marvel to cease attracting admiring glances, and turn into a household object which we wouldn't hesitate to condemn were we to suffer at its hands the minor inconvenience of a delayed *glace au chocolat*.

It points clearly enough to the problems faced by human beings, comparatively humdrum things, in seeking eternal, or at least lifelong, appreciation from their fellows.

Q: How long can the average human expect to be appreciated?
A: Fully appreciated? Often, as little as quarter of an hour. As a boy, Proust's narrator longs to befriend the beautiful vivacious Gilberte, who he has met playing in the Champs-Élysées. Eventually, his wish comes true, Gilberte becomes his friend and invites him regularly to tea at her house. There she cuts him slices of cake, ministers to his needs and treats him with great affection.

He is happy, but soon enough, not as happy as he should be. For so long, the idea of having tea in Gilberte's house was like a vague chimerical dream, but after a quarter of an hour in her drawing room, it is the time before he knew her, before she was cutting him cake and showering him with affection, that starts to grow chimerical and vague.

The outcome can only be a certain blindness to the favours he is enjoying, he will soon forget *what* there is to be grateful for because the memory of Gilberte-less life will fade, and with it, evidence of what there is to savour. The smile on Gilberte's face, the luxury of her tea and the warmth of her manners will eventually become such a familiar part of his life that there will be as much incentive to notice them as there is to notice ubiquitous elements like trees, clouds or telephones.

The reason for this neglect is that like all of us in the Proustian conception, the narrator is a creature of habit, and therefore always liable to grow contemptuous of what is familiar.

> We only really know what is new, what suddenly introduces to our sensibility a change of tone which strikes us, that for which habit has not yet substituted its pale facsimiles.

Q: Why does habit have such a dulling effect?
A: Proust's most suggestive answer lies in a passing remark about the Biblical Noah and his Ark.

> When I was a small child, no character in the Bible seemed to me to have a worse fate than Noah, because of the flood which kept him locked up in the Ark for forty days. Later on, I was often ill, and also had to stay in an 'Ark' for endless days. It was then I understood that Noah would never have been able to see the world as

well as from the Ark, even though it was shuttered and it was night on earth.

How could Noah have seen anything of the planet when he was sitting in a shuttered Ark with an amphibious zoo? Though we usually assume that seeing an object requires us to have visual contact with it, and that seeing a mountain involves visiting the Alps and opening our eyes, this may only be the first, and in a sense the inferior, part of seeing, for appreciating an object properly may also require us to recreate it in our mind's eye.

After looking at a mountain, if we shut our lids and dwell on the scene internally we are led to seize on its important details, the mass of visual information is interpreted and the mountain's salient features identified: its granite peaks, its glacial indentations, the mist hovering above the tree line; details which we would previously have *seen* but not for that matter *noticed*.

Though Noah was six hundred years old when God flooded the world, and would have had much time to look at his surroundings, the fact that they were always there, that they were so permanent in his visual field, would have given him no encouragement to recreate them internally. What was the point of focusing closely on a bush in his mind's eye when there was abundant physical evidence of bushes in the vicinity?

How different the situation would have been after two weeks in the Ark, when, nostalgic for his old surroundings, and unable to see them, Noah would naturally have begun to focus on the memory of bushes, trees and mountains, and therefore, for the first time in his six-hundred-year life, begun to see them properly.

It suggests that having something physically present sets up far from ideal circumstances in which to notice it. Presence may in fact be the very element that encourages us to ignore or neglect it, because we feel we have done all the work simply in securing visual contact.

Q: Should we spend more time locked up in Arks, then?
A: It *would* help us pay more attention to things, lovers in particular. Deprivation quickly drives us into a process of appreciation, which is not to say that we *have* to be deprived in order to appreciate things, but rather that we should learn a lesson from what we naturally do when we lack something, and apply it to conditions where we don't.

If long acquaintance with a lover so often breeds boredom, breeds a sense of knowing a person too well, the problem may ironically be that we do not know them well enough. Whereas the initial novelty of the relationship could leave us in no doubt as to our ignorance, the subsequent reliable physical presence of the lover and the routines of communal life can delude us into thinking that we have achieved genuine, and dull familiarity; whereas it may be no more than a fake sense of familiarity which physical presence fosters, and which Noah would have felt for six hundred years in relation to the world, until the Flood taught him otherwise.

Q: Did Proust have any relevant thoughts on dating? What should one talk about on a first date? And is it good to wear black?

A: Advice is scant. A more fundamental doubt is whether one should accept dinner in the first place.

> There is no doubt that a person's charms are less frequently a cause of love than a remark such as: 'No, this evening I shan't be free.'

If this response proves bewitching, it is because of the connection made in Noah's case between appreciation and absence. Though a person may be filled with attributes, an incentive is nevertheless required to ensure that a seducer will focus wholeheartedly on these, an incentive which finds perfect form in a dinner rebuff, the dating equivalent of forty days at sea.

Proust demonstrates the benefits of delay in his thoughts on the appreciation of clothes. Both Albertine and the Duchesse de Guermantes are interested in fashion. However, Albertine has very little money and the Duchesse owns half of France. The Duchesse's wardrobes are therefore overflowing, as soon as she sees something she wants she can send for the dressmaker and her desire is fulfilled as rapidly as hands can sew. Albertine on the other hand can hardly buy anything, and has to think at length before she does so. She spends hours studying clothes, dreaming of a particular coat or hat or dressing gown.

The result is that, though Albertine has far fewer clothes than the Duchesse, her understanding, appreciation and *love* of them is far greater:

Like every obstacle in the way of possessing something
. . . poverty, more generous than opulence, gives women
far more than the clothes they cannot afford to buy: the
desire for those clothes, which creates a genuine, detailed,
thorough knowledge of them.

Proust compares Albertine to a student who visits Dresden
after cultivating a desire to see a particular painting, whereas
the Duchesse is like a wealthy tourist who travels without
any desire or knowledge, and experiences nothing but bewilderment, boredom and exhaustion when she arrives.

It emphasizes the extent to which physical possession is
only one component of appreciation. If the rich are fortunate
in being able to travel to Dresden as soon as the desire to do
so arises, or buy a dress just after they have seen it in a
catalogue, they are cursed because of the speed with which
their wealth fulfils their desires. No sooner have they
thought of Dresden than they can be on a train there, no
sooner have they seen a dress than it can be in their wardrobe.
They therefore have no opportunity to suffer the interval
between desire and gratification which the less privileged
endure, and which, for all its apparent unpleasantness, has
the incalculable benefit of allowing people to know and fall
deeply in love with paintings in Dresden, hats, dressing
gowns and someone who isn't free this evening.

Q: Was he against sex before marriage?
A: No, just before love. And not for any starched reasons,
simply because he felt it wasn't a good idea to sleep

together when encouraging someone to fall in love was a consideration:

> Women who are to some extent resistant, whom one cannot possess at once, whom one does not even know at first whether one will ever possess, are the only interesting ones.

Q: Surely not?
A: Other women may of course be fascinating, the problem is that they risk not *seeming* so, given what the Duchesse de Guermantes has told us about the consequences of acquiring beautiful things too easily.

Take the case of prostitutes, a group more or less available every night. As a young man, Proust had been a compulsive masturbator, so compulsive that his father had urged him to go to a brothel, to take his mind off what the nineteenth century considered to be a highly dangerous pastime. In a candid letter to his grandfather, sixteen-year-old Marcel described how the visit had gone:

> I so badly needed to see a woman in order to stop my bad habits of masturbating that papa gave me 10 francs to go to the brothel. But, 1st in my excitement, I broke the chamber pot, 3 francs, 2nd in this same excitement, I wasn't able to have sex. So now I'm back to square one, constantly waiting for another 10 francs to empty myself and for 3 more francs for that pot.

But the brothel trip was more than a practical disaster; it revealed a conceptual problem with prostitution. The prostitute is in an unfortunate position in the Proustian theory of desire, because she both wishes to entice a man and yet is commercially prevented from doing what is most likely to encourage love, namely, tell him that she is not free tonight. She may be clever and attractive, and yet the one thing she cannot do is foster doubts as to whether or not he will ever possess her physically. The outcome is clear, and therefore real lasting desire unlikely.

> If prostitutes . . . attract us so little, it is not because they are less beautiful than other women, but because they are ready and waiting; because they already offer us precisely what we seek to attain.

Q: So he believed that sex was everything men wanted to attain?
A: A further distinction might have to be made. The prostitute offers a man what he *thinks* he wants to attain, she gives him an illusion of attainment, but one which is nevertheless strong enough to threaten the gestation of love.

To return to the Duchesse, she fails to appreciate her dresses not because they are less beautiful than other dresses, but because *physical possession* is so easy, which fools her into thinking that she has acquired everything she wanted, and distracts her from pursuing the only real form of possession which is effective in Proust's eyes, namely, *imaginative possession* [dwelling on the details of the dress, the folds of the material, the delicacy of the thread], an imaginative possession which Albertine already pursues, through no conscious choice, because it is a natural response to being denied physical contact.

Q: Does this mean he didn't think much of making love?
A: He merely thought humans were missing an anatomical part with which to perform the act properly. In the Proustian scheme, it is impossible to love someone *physically*. Given the coyness of his age, he limited his thoughts to the disappointment of kissing.

> Man, a creature clearly less rudimentary than the sea urchin or even the whale, nevertheless lacks a certain number of essential organs, and particularly possesses none that will serve for kissing. For this absent organ he substitutes his lips, and perhaps he thereby achieves a result slightly more satisfying than caressing his beloved with a horny tusk. But a pair of lips, designed to convey to the palate the taste of whatever whets their appetite, must be content, without understanding their mistake or admitting their disappointment, with roaming over the surface and with coming to a halt at the barrier of the impenetrable but irresistible cheek.

Why do we kiss people? At one level, merely to generate the pleasurable sensation of rubbing an area of nerve endings against a corresponding strip of soft, fleshy, moist skin tissue. However, the hopes with which we approach the prospect of an initial kiss typically extend beyond this. We seek to hold and savour not just a mouth but an entire beloved person. With the kiss we hope to achieve a higher form of possession; the longing a beloved inspires in us promises to come to an end once our lips are allowed to roam freely over theirs.

However for Proust, though a kiss can produce a pleasurable physical tingle, it cannot grant us a true sense of amorous possession.

For example, his narrator is attracted to Albertine, who he met as she walked along the Normandy coast one brilliant summer's day. He is attracted to her rosy cheeks, her black hair, her beauty spot, her impudent, confident manner, and to things she evokes and makes him nostalgic for: the summer, the smell of the sea, youth. Once he returns to Paris after the summer, Albertine comes to his flat. In contrast to her reserve when he tried to kiss her at the seaside, she now lies close to him on the bed and falls into an embrace. It promises to be a moment of resolution. Yet whereas he had hoped that the kiss would allow him to savour Albertine, her past, the beach, the summer and the circumstances of their meeting, the reality is somewhat more prosaic. His lips brushing against Albertine's allow him as much contact with her as a brush with a horny tusk. He can't see her, because of the awkwardness of the kissing position, and his nose is so squashed he can hardly breathe.

It may have been a particularly inept kiss, but by detailing its disappointments Proust points to a general difficulty in a physical method of appreciation. The narrator recognizes that he could do almost anything physically with Albertine, take her on his knees, hold her head in his hands, caress her, but that he would still be doing nothing other than touching the sealed envelope of a far more elusive, beloved person.

This might not matter were it not for a tendency to believe that physical contact might in fact put us directly in touch with the object of our love. Disappointed with the kiss, the risk is that we would then ascribe our disappointment to the tedium of the person we were kissing rather than to the limitations involved in doing so.

Q: Are there any secrets to long-lasting relationships?
A: Infidelity. Not the act itself, but the threat of it. For Proust, an injection of jealousy is the only thing capable of rescuing a relationship ruined by habit. A word of advice for someone who has taken the fatal step of cohabitation:

> When you come to live with a woman, you will soon cease to see anything of what made you love her; though it is true that the two sundered elements can be reunited by jealousy.

Nevertheless, the characters in Proust's novel are inept at capitalizing on their jealousy. The threat of losing their partner may lead them to realize that they have not appreciated this person adequately, but because they only understand physical appreciation, they do no more than secure physical allegiance, which merely brings temporary relief before boredom sets in again. They are forced into a debilitating vicious circle; they desire someone, kiss them with a horny tusk and get bored. If someone threatens the relationship, they get jealous, wake up for a moment, have another kiss with the horny tusk and get bored once more.

Condensed in a male heterosexual version, the situation runs like this:

> Afraid of losing her, we forget all the others. Sure of keeping her, we compare her with those others whom at once we prefer to her.

Q: So what would Proust have told these unhappy lovers if he had been able to meet and help them, as he had boasted to André Gide?
A: At a guess, he would have sent them to think about Noah and the world he could suddenly see from his Ark, and the Duchesse de Guermantes and the dresses she had never looked at properly in her wardrobe.

Q: But what would he have said to Swann and Odette in particular?
A: A fine question – but perhaps there are limits to how far one can ignore the lesson of perhaps the wisest person in Proust's book, a certain Mme Leroi, who, when asked for her views on love, curtly replies:

> 'Love? I make it often, but I never talk about it.'

CHAPTER NINE

HOW TO PUT
BOOKS DOWN

How seriously should we take books? 'Dear friend,' Proust told André Gide, 'I believe, contrary to the fashion among our contemporaries, that one can have a very lofty idea of literature, and at the same time have a good-natured laugh at it.' The remark may have been throwaway, but its underlying message was not. For a man who devoted his life to literature, Proust manifested a singular awareness of the dangers of taking books too seriously, or rather of adopting a fetishistically reverent attitude towards them, which while appearing to pay due homage would in fact travesty the spirit of literary production; a healthy relationship to other people's books would depend as much on an appreciation of their limitations as of their benefits.

i. The benefits of reading

In 1899 things were going badly for Proust. He was twenty-eight, he had done nothing with his life, he was still living at home, he had never earned any money, he was always ill and worst of all, he had been trying to write a novel for the last four years and it was showing few signs of working out. In the autumn of that year, he went on holiday to the French Alps, to the spa town of Évian, and it was here that he read and fell in love with the works of John Ruskin, the English art critic renowned for his writings on Venice, Turner, the Italian Renaissance, Gothic architecture and Alpine landscapes.

Proust's encounter with Ruskin exemplified the benefits of reading. 'The universe suddenly regained infinite value in my eyes,' explained Proust subsequently; because the universe had had such value in Ruskin's eyes, and because he had been a genius at transmuting his impressions into words. Ruskin had expressed things which Proust might have felt himself, but could not have articulated on his own; in Ruskin, he found experiences which he had never been more than semi-conscious of, raised and beautifully assembled in language.

Ruskin sensitized Proust to the visible world, to architecture, art and nature. Here is Ruskin awakening his readers' senses to a few of the many things going on in an ordinary mountain stream:

> If it meets a rock three or four feet above the level of its bed, it will often neither part nor foam, nor express any concern about the matter, but clear it in a smooth dome of water, without apparent exertion, the whole surface of the surge being drawn into parallel lines by its extreme velocity, so that the whole river has the appearance of a deep and raging sea, with only this difference, that torrent-waves always break backwards, and sea-waves forwards. Thus, then, in the water which has gained an impetus, we have the most exquisite arrangements of curved lines, perpetually changing from convex to con-

cave, and vice versa, following every swell and hollow of
the bed with their modulating grace, and all in unison
of motion, presenting perhaps the most beautiful series
of inorganic forms which nature can possibly produce.

Aside from landscape, Ruskin helped Proust to discover the
beauty of the great cathedrals of northern France. When he
returned to Paris after his holiday, Proust travelled to
Bourges and to Chartres, to Amiens and Rouen. Later
explaining what Ruskin had taught him, Proust pointed to
a passage on Rouen cathedral in *The Seven Lamps of
Architecture*, in which Ruskin minutely described a particular stone figure which had been carved, together with
hundreds of others, in one of the cathedral's portals. The
figure was of a little man, no more than ten centimetres
high, with a vexed, puzzled expression, and one hand
pressed hard against his cheek, wrinkling the flesh under
his eye.

For Proust, Ruskin's concern for the little man had effected
a kind of resurrection, one characteristic of great art. He
had known how to look at this figure, and had hence
brought it back to life for succeeding generations. Ever
polite, Proust offered a playful apology to the little figure
for what would have been his own inability to notice him
without Ruskin as a guide ['I would not have been clever
enough to find you, amongst the thousands of stones in our
towns, to pick out your figure, to rediscover your personality, to summon you, to make you live again']. It was a

symbol of what Ruskin had done for Proust, and what all books might do for their readers, namely bring back to life, from the deadness caused by habit and inattention, valuable yet neglected aspects of experience.

Because he had been so impressed by Ruskin, Proust sought to extend his contact with him by engaging in the traditional occupation open to those who love reading: literary scholarship. He set aside his novelistic projects and became a Ruskin scholar. When the English critic died in 1900, he wrote his obituary, followed it up with several essays, and then undertook the immense task of translating Ruskin into French, a task all the more ambitious because he hardly spoke any English and, according to Georges de Lauris, would have had trouble correctly ordering a lamb chop in English in a restaurant. However, he succeeded in producing highly accurate translations of both Ruskin's *Bible of Amiens* and his *Sesame and Lilies*, adding an array of scholarly footnotes testifying to the breadth of his Ruskinian knowledge. It was work he carried out with the fanaticism and rigour of a maniacal professor; in the words of his friend Marie Nordlinger:

> The apparent discomfort in which he worked was quite incredible; the bed was littered with books and papers, his pillows were all over the place, a bamboo table on his left was piled high, and more often than not, there was no support for whatever he was writing on (no wonder he wrote illegibly), with a cheap wooden penholder or two lying where it had fallen on the floor.

Because Proust was such a good scholar and such an unsuccessful novelist, an academic career must have beckoned. It was his mother's hope. After watching him waste years on a novel that had gone nowhere, she took pleasure in discovering that her son had the makings of a fine scholar. Proust could not have ignored his own aptitude and indeed, many years later, expressed sympathy with his mother's judgement:

> I always agreed with Maman that I could have done only one thing in life, but a thing which we both valued so much that it is saying a lot: namely, an excellent professor.

ii. The limitations of reading

However, needless to say, Proust did not become Professor Proust, Ruskin scholar and translator, a significant fact, given how well suited he was to academic discipline, how ill suited he was to almost everything else and how much he respected his beloved mother's judgement.

His reservations could hardly have been more subtle. He was in no doubt as to the immense value of reading and study, and could defend his Ruskinian labours against any vulgar arguments in favour of mental self-sufficiency.

> The mediocre usually imagine that to let ourselves be guided by the books we admire robs our faculty of

judgement of part of its independence. 'What can it matter to you what Ruskin feels: feel for yourself.' Such a view rests on a psychological error which will be discounted by all those who have accepted a spiritual discipline and feel thereby that their power of understanding and of feeling is infinitely enhanced, and their critical sense never paralysed . . . There is no better way of coming to be aware of what one feels oneself than by trying to recreate in oneself what a master has felt. In this profound effort it is our thought itself that we bring out into the light, together with his.

Yet something in this forceful defence of reading and scholarship intimated Proust's reservations. Without drawing attention to how contentious or critical the point was, he argued that we should be reading for a particular reason; not to pass the time, not out of detached curiosity, not out of a dispassionate wish to find out what Ruskin felt, but because, to go back with italics, 'there is no better way of coming to be aware of *what one feels oneself* than by trying to recreate in oneself what a master has felt'. We should read other people's books in order to learn what *we* feel, it is our own thoughts we should be developing even if it is another writer's thoughts which help us do so. A fulfilled academic life would therefore require us to judge that the writers we were studying articulated in their books a sufficient range of our own concerns, and that in the act of understanding them through translation or commentary, we would simultaneously be understanding and developing the spiritually significant parts of themselves.

And herein lay Proust's problem, because in his view, books could not make us aware of enough of the things we felt. They might open our eyes, sensitize us, enhance our powers of perception, but at a certain point they would stop, not by coincidence, not occasionally, not out of bad luck, but inevitably, by definition, for the stark and simple reason that *the author wasn't us*. There would come a moment with every book when we would feel that something was incongruous, misunderstood or constraining, and it would give us a responsibility to leave our guide behind and continue our thoughts alone. Proust's respect for Ruskin was enormous, but having worked intensely on his texts for six years, having lived with bits of paper scattered across his bed and his bamboo table piled high with books, in a particular burst of irritation at continually being tethered to another man's words, Proust exclaimed that Ruskin's qualities had not prevented him from frequently being 'silly, maniacal, constraining, false and ridiculous'.

The fact that Proust did not at this point turn to translating George Eliot or annotating Dostoevsky signals a recognition that the frustration he felt with Ruskin was not incidental to this author, but reflected a universally constraining dimension to reading and scholarship, and was sufficient reason never to strive for the title of Professor Proust.

It is one of the great and wonderful characteristics of good books (which allows us to see the role, at once essential yet limited, that reading may play in our spiritual lives) that for the author they may be called 'Conclusions' but for the reader 'Incitements'. We feel very strongly that our own wisdom begins where that of the author leaves off, and we would like him to provide us with answers when all he is able to do is provide us with desires . . . That is the value of reading, and also its inadequacy. To make it into a discipline is to give too large a role to what is only an incitement. Reading is on the threshold of the spiritual life; it can introduce us to it: it does not constitute it.

*

However, Proust was singularly aware of how tempting it was to believe that reading could constitute our entire spiritual life, which led him to formulate some careful lines of instruction on a responsible approach to books:

> As long as reading is for us the instigator whose magic keys have opened the door to those dwelling-places deep within us that we would not have known how to enter, its role in our lives is salutary. It becomes dangerous, on the other hand, when, instead of awakening us to the personal life of the mind, reading tends to take its place, when the truth no longer appears to us as an ideal which we can realize only by the intimate progress of our own thought and the efforts of our heart, but as something material, deposited between the leaves of books like a honey fully prepared by others and which we need only take the trouble to reach down from the shelves of

libraries and then sample passively in a perfect repose of mind and body.

Because books are so good at helping us become aware of certain things we feel, Proust recognized the ease with which we could be tempted to leave the entire task of interpreting our lives to these objects.

He gave an example in his novel of such excessive reliance in a vignette about a man reading the works of La Bruyère. He pictured him coming across the following aphorism in the pages of *Les Caractères*:

> Men often want to love, without managing to do so: they seek their own ruin without being able to attain it, and, if I can put it thus, they are forced against their will to remain free.

Because this suitor had tried unsuccessfully for years to make himself loved by a woman who would only have made him unhappy if she *had* loved him, Proust conjectured that the link between his own life and the aphorism would deeply move this unfortunate character. He would now read the passage over and over again, swelling it with meaning until it was ready to burst, appending to the aphorism a million words and the most stirring memories of his own life, repeating it with immense joy because it seemed so beautiful and so true.

Though it was undoubtedly a crystallization of many aspects

of this man's experience, Proust implied that such extreme enthusiasm for La Bruyère's thought would at some point distract the man from the particularities of his own feelings. The aphorism might have helped him to understand part of his story, but it did not reflect it exactly; in order fully to capture his romantic misfortunes, the sentence would have had to read, 'Men often want *to be* loved . . .' rather than 'Men often want *to love* . . .' It wasn't a major difference, but it was a symbol of the way that books, even when they brilliantly articulate some of our experiences, may nevertheless leave others behind.

It obligates us to read with care, to welcome the insights books give us, but not to subjugate our independence, or smother the nuances of our own love life in the process.

Otherwise, we might suffer a range of symptoms which Proust identified in the overreverent, overreliant reader:

Symptom no. 1: That we mistake writers for oracles

As a boy, Proust had loved reading Théophile Gautier. Certain sentences in Gautier's *Le Capitaine Fracasse* had seemed so profound that he had started to think of the author as an extraordinary figure of limitless insight, who he would have wanted to consult on all his significant problems:

> I would have wished for him, the one wise custodian of the truth, to tell me what I ought rightly to think of

Shakespeare, of Saintine, of Sophocles, of Euripides, of Silvio Pellico . . . Above all, I would have wished him to tell me whether I would have had a better chance of arriving at the truth by repeating my first-form year at school, or by becoming a diplomat or a barrister at the Court of Appeal.

Sadly, Gautier's inspiring, fascinating sentences had a habit of coming in the midst of some very tedious passages, in which the author would, for instance, spend an age describing a château, and show no interest in telling Marcel what to think of Sophocles, or whether he should go into the Foreign Office or the law.

It was probably a good thing, as far as Marcel's career was concerned. Gautier's capacity for insights in one area did not necessarily mean that he was capable of worthwhile insights in another. Yet how natural to feel that someone who has been extremely lucid on certain topics might turn out to be a perfect authority on other topics too, might indeed turn out to have the answers to *everything*.

Many of the exaggerated hopes which Proust harboured of Gautier as a boy came in time to be harboured of him. There were people who believed that he too might solve the riddle of existence, a wild hope presumably derived from the evidence of nothing more than his novel. The staff of *L'Intransigeant*, those inspired journalists who had felt it appropriate to consult Proust on the consequences of global apocalypse, were supreme believers in the oracular wisdom of writers, and repeatedly bothered Proust with their questions. For example, they felt he might be the perfect person to answer this enquiry:

> If for some reason you were forced to take up a manual profession, which one would you choose, according to your tastes, your aptitudes and your capacities?

'I think I would become a baker. It is an honourable thing to give people their daily bread,' replied Proust, who was incapable of making a piece of toast, after asserting that writing in any case constituted manual labour: 'You make a distinction between manual and spiritual professions which I couldn't subscribe to. The spirit guides the hand' – which Céleste, whose job it was to clean the loo, might politely have contested.

It was a nonsensical reply, but then again, it was a nonsensical question, at least when addressed to Proust. Why would an ability to write *In Search of Lost Time* in any way indicate an aptitude for advising recently dismissed white-collar workers on their career? Why would the readers of *L'Intransigeant* need to be exposed to misleading notions of the baking life, put forward by a man who had never had a proper job and didn't much like bread? Why not let Proust answer the questions in his area of competence, and otherwise admit the need for a well-qualified career adviser?

Symptom no. 2: That we will be unable to write after reading a good book

This may seem a narrowly professional consideration, but it has wider relevance if one imagines that a good book might also stop us from thinking ourselves, because it would strike us as so perfect, as so inherently superior to anything our own minds could come up with. In short, a good book might silence us.

Reading Proust nearly silenced Virginia Woolf. She loved his novel, but loved it rather too much. There wasn't *enough* wrong with it, a crushing recognition when one follows Walter Benjamin in his assessment of why people become writers: because they are unable to find a book already written which they are completely happy with. And the difficulty for Virginia was that, for a time at least, she thought she had found one.

Marcel and Virginia – A short story

Virginia Woolf first mentioned Proust in a letter she wrote to Roger Fry in the autumn of 1919. He was in France, she was in Richmond, where the weather was foggy and the garden in bad shape, and she casually asked him whether he might bring her back a copy of *Swann's Way* on his return.

It was 1922 before she next mentioned Proust. She had turned forty and, despite the entreaty to Fry, still hadn't read anything of Proust's work, though in a letter to E. M. Forster, she revealed that others in the vicinity were being more diligent. 'Everyone is reading Proust. I sit silent and hear their reports. It seems to be a tremendous experience,' she explained, though appeared to be procrastinating out of a fear of being overwhelmed by something in the novel, an object she referred to more as if it were a swamp than hundreds of bits of paper stuck together with thread and glue; 'I'm shivering on the brink, and waiting to be submerged with a horrid sort of notion that I shall go down and down and down and perhaps never come up again.'

She took the plunge nevertheless, and the problems started. As she told Roger Fry, 'Proust so titillates my own desire for expression that I can hardly set out the sentence. "Oh, if I could write like that!" I cry. And at the moment such is the astonishing vibration and saturation that he procures – there's something sexual in it – that I feel I *can* write like that, and seize my pen, and then I *can't* write like that.'

In what sounded like a celebration of *In Search of Lost Time*, but was in fact a far darker verdict on her future as a writer, she told Fry: 'My great adventure is really Proust. Well – what remains to be written after that? . . . How, at last, has someone solidified what has always escaped – and made it too into this beautiful and perfectly enduring substance? One has to put the book down and gasp.'

In spite of the gasping, Woolf realized that *Mrs Dalloway* still remained to be written, after which she allowed herself a brief burst of elation at the thought that she might have produced something decent. 'I wonder if this time I have achieved something?' she asked herself in her diary, but the pleasure was short-lived: 'Well, nothing anyhow compared with Proust, in whom I am embedded now. The thing about Proust is his combination of the utmost sensibility with the utmost tenacity. He searches out these butterfly shades to the last grain. He is as tough as catgut and as evanescent as a butterfly's bloom. And he will I suppose both influence me and make me out of temper with every sentence of my own.'

But Woolf knew how to hate her sentences well enough even without Proust's assistance. 'So sick of *Orlando* I can write nothing,' she told her diary shortly after completing this book in 1928. 'I have corrected the proofs in a week: and cannot spin another phrase. I detest my own volubility. Why be always spouting words?'

However, any bad mood she was in was liable to take a dramatic plunge for the worse after the briefest contact with the Frenchman. The diary entry continued: 'Take up Proust after dinner and put him down. This is the worst time of all. It makes me suicidal. Nothing seems left to do. All seems insipid and worthless.'

Nevertheless, she didn't yet commit suicide, though she did take the wise step of ceasing to read Proust, and was therefore able to write a few more books whose sentences were neither insipid nor worthless. Then in 1934, when she was working on *The Years*, there was a sign that she had at last freed herself from Proust's shadow. She told Ethel Smyth that she had picked up *In Search of Lost Time* again, 'which is of course so magnificent that I can't write myself within its arc. For years I've put off finishing it; but now, thinking I may die one of these years, I've returned, and let my own scribble do what it likes. Lord, what a hopeless bad book mine will be!'

The tone suggests that Woolf had at last made her peace with Proust. He could have his terrain, she had hers to scribble in. The path from depression and self-loathing to cheerful defiance suggests a gradual recognition that one person's achievements did not have to invalidate another's, that there would always be something left to do even if it momentarily appeared otherwise. Proust might have expressed many things well, but independent thought and the history of the novel had not come to a halt with him. His book did not have to be followed by silence, there was still space for the scribbling of others, for *Mrs Dalloway*, *The Common Reader*, *A Room of One's Own*, and in particular there was space for what these books symbolized in this context, perceptions of one's own.

Symptom no. 3: That we become artistic idolaters

Aside from the danger of overvaluing writers and undervaluing oneself, there is a risk that we will revere artists for the wrong reasons, indulging in what Proust called artistic idolatry. In the religious context, idolatry suggests a fixation on an aspect of religion – on an image of a worshipped deity, on a particular law or holy book – which distracts us from, and even contravenes, the overall spirit of the religion.

Proust suggested that a structurally similar problem existed in art, where artistic idolaters combined a literal reverence for objects depicted in art with a neglect of the spirit of art. They would, for instance, become particularly attached to a part of the countryside depicted by a great painter, and mistake this for an appreciation of the painter, they would focus on the objects *in* a picture, as opposed to the spirit *of* the picture – whereas the essence of Proust's aesthetic position was contained in the deceptively simple yet momentous assertion that 'a picture's beauty does not depend on the things portrayed in it'.

Proust accused his friend, the aristocrat and poet Robert de Montesquiou, of artistic idolatry, because of the pleasure he took whenever he encountered in life an object which had been depicted by an artist. Montesquiou would gush if he happened to see one of his female friends wearing a dress like that which Balzac had imagined for the character of the Princesse de Cadignan in his novel *Les Secrets de la Princesse de Cadignan*. Why was this type of delight idolatrous? Because Montesquiou's enthusiasm had nothing to do with an appreciation of the dress and everything to do with a respect for Balzac's name. Montesquiou had no reasons of his own for liking the dress, he hadn't assimilated the principles of Balzac's aesthetic vision, nor grasped the *general* lesson latent in Balzac's appreciation of this *particular* object. Problems would therefore arise as soon as Montesquiou was faced with a dress which Balzac had never had a chance to describe, and which Montesquiou would perhaps ignore – even though Balzac, and a good Balzacian, would no doubt have been able to evaluate the merits of each dress appropriately had they been in his shoes.

Symptom no. 4: That we will be tempted to invest in a copy of La Cuisine Retrouvée

Food has a privileged role in Proust's writings; it is often lovingly described and appreciatively eaten. To name but a few of the many dishes which Proust parades past his readers, we can cite a cheese soufflé, a string bean salad, a trout with almonds, a grilled red mullet, a bouillabaisse, a skate in black butter, a beef casserole, some lamb with a Béarnaise sauce, a beef Stroganoff, a bowl of stewed peaches, a raspberry mousse, a madeleine, an apricot tart, an apple tart, a raisin cake, a chocolate sauce and a chocolate soufflé.

The contrast between what we usually eat and the mouth-watering nature of the food Proust's characters enjoy might inspire us to try and savour these Proustian dishes more directly. In which case, it could be tempting to acquire a copy of a glossily illustrated cookbook entitled *La Cuisine Retrouvée*, which contains recipes for every dish mentioned in Proust's work, is compiled by a top Parisian chef and was first published in 1991 [by a company otherwise responsible for a comparably useful title, *Les Carnets de Cuisine de Monet*]. It would enable a moderately competent cook to pay extraordinary homage to the great novelist, and perhaps gain a closer understanding of Proust's art. It would, for instance, enable a dedicated Proustian to produce exactly the kind of chocolate mousse which Françoise served to the narrator and his family in Combray.

Françoise's Chocolate Mousse

Ingredients: 100g of plain cooking chocolate, 100g of caster sugar, half a litre of milk, six eggs.

Method: Bring the milk to the boil, add the chocolate broken in pieces, and let it melt gently, stirring the mixture with a wooden spoon. Whip the sugar with the yolks of the six eggs. Preheat the oven to 130°C.

When the chocolate has completely melted, pour it over the eggs and the sugar, mix rapidly and energetically, then pass through a strainer.

Pour out the liquid into little ramekins 8cm in diameter, and put into the oven, in a bain-marie, for an hour. Leave to cool before serving.

But once the recipe had resulted in a delicious dessert, in between mouthfuls of Françoise's chocolate mousse, we might pause to ask whether this dish, and by extension the entire volume of *La Cuisine Retrouvée*, really constituted a homage to Proust, or whether it was not in danger of encouraging the very sin which he had warned his readers about, artistic idolatry. Though Proust might have welcomed the principle of a cookbook based on his work, the question is what form he would have wished it to take. To accept his arguments about artistic idolatry would mean recognizing that the particular foods which featured in his novel were irrelevant when compared to the spirit in which the food was considered, a transferable spirit which owed nothing to the exact chocolate mousse which Françoise had prepared, or the particular bouillabaisse which Mme Verdurin had served at her table – and might be as relevant when approaching a bowl of muesli, a curry or a paella.

The danger is that *La Cuisine Retrouvée* will unwittingly throw us into depression the day we fail to find the right ingredients for the chocolate mousse or green bean salad, and are forced to eat a hamburger – which Proust never had a chance to write about.

It wouldn't, of course, have been Marcel's intention: a picture's beauty does not depend on the things portrayed in it.

Symptom no. 5: That we will be tempted to visit Illiers-Combray

Travelling by car southwest of the cathedral town of Chartres, the view through the windscreen is of a familiar northern European arable landscape. One could be anywhere, the only feature of note being a flatness to the earth which lends disproportionate significance to the occasional water tower or agricultural silo asserting itself on the horizon above the windscreen wipers. The monotony is a welcome break from the effort of looking at interesting things, a time to rearrange the twisted accordion-shaped Michelin map before reaching the chateaux of the Loire, or to digest the sight of Chartres cathedral with its claw-like flying buttresses and weather-worn bell-towers. The smaller roads cut through villages whose houses are shuttered for a siesta that appears to last all day; even the petrol stations show no sign of life, their Elf flags flapping in a wind blowing in from across vast wheatfields. A Citroën makes an occasional hasty appearance in the rear-view mirror, then overtakes with exaggerated impatience, as if speed was the only way to protest against the desperate monotony.

At the larger junctions, sitting innocuously among signs vainly asserting a speed limit of ninety and pointing the way to Tours and Le Mans, the motorist may notice a metal arrow indicating the distance to the small town of Illiers-Combray. For centuries, the sign pointed simply to Illiers, but in 1971 the town chose to let even the least cultured motorist know of its connection to its most famous son, or rather visitor. For it was here that Proust spent his summers from the age of six until nine and once again at the age of fifteen, in the house of his father's sister, Elisabeth Amiot – and here that he drew inspiration for the creation of his fictional Combray.

There is something eerie about driving into a town which has surrendered part of its claim to independent reality in favour of a role fashioned for it by a novelist who once spent a few summers there as a boy in the late nineteenth century. But Illiers-Combray appears to relish the idea. In a corner of the Rue du Docteur Proust, the pâtisserie-confiserie hangs a large, somewhat puzzling sign outside its door: 'The House where Aunt Léonie used to buy her madeleines.'

Competition is fierce with the boulangerie in the Place du Marché, for it too is involved in the *'fabrication de la petite madeleine de Marcel Proust'*. A packet of eight can be had for twenty francs, twelve for thirty. The boulanger – who hasn't read it – knows that the shop would have had to close long ago had it not been for *In Search of Lost Time*, which draws customers in from across the world. They can be seen with cameras and madeleine bags, heading for the house of tante Amiot, an undistinguished, rather sombre edifice that would be unlikely to detain one's attention were it not for the fact that within its walls young Proust once collected impressions used to build the narrator's bedroom, the kitchen where Françoise prepared her chocolate mousse and the garden gate through which Swann came for dinner.

Inside, there is the hushed, semi-religious feel reminiscent of a church, children grow quiet and expectant, the guide gives them a warm if pitying smile while their mothers remind them to touch nothing along the way. There turns out to be little temptation. The rooms recreate in its full aesthetic horror the feel of a tastelessly furnished, provincial bourgeois nineteenth-century home. Inside a giant perspex display cabinet on top of a table next to 'tante Léonie's bed' the curators have placed a white teacup, an ancient bottle of Vichy water and a solitary, curiously oily-looking madeleine, which on closer inspection reveals itself to be made of plastic.

According to Monsieur Larcher, the author of a leaflet on sale at the tourist office,

> If one wishes to grasp the deep and occult sense of *In Search of Lost Time*, one must, before starting to read it, devote an entire day to visiting Illiers-Combray. The magic of Combray can really only be experienced in this privileged place.

Though Larcher displays admirable civic feeling and would no doubt be applauded by every patissier involved in the madeleine trade, one wonders after such a day whether he is not at risk of exaggerating the qualities of his town, and unwittingly diminishing those of Proust.

More honest visitors will admit to themselves that there is nothing striking about the town. It looks much like any other, which doesn't mean it is uninteresting, simply that there is no obvious evidence of the privileged status which Monsieur Larcher accords it. It is a fitting Proustian point: the interest of a town is necessarily dependent on a certain way of looking at it. Combray may be pleasant, but it is as valuable a place to visit as any in the large plateau of northern France, the beauty which Proust revealed there could be present, latent, in almost any town, if only we made the effort to consider it in a Proustian way.

Ironically, however, it is out of an idolatrous reverence for Proust, and a misunderstanding of his aesthetic ideas, that we speed blindly through the surrounding countryside, through neighbouring non-literary towns and villages like Brou, Bonneval and Courville, on our way to the imagined delights of Proust's childhood locale. In so doing, we forget that had Proust's family settled in Courville, or his old aunt taken up residence in Bonneval, it would have been to these places that we would have driven, just as unfairly. Our pilgrimage is idolatrous because it privileges the place Proust happened to grow up in rather than his manner of considering it, an oversight which the corpulent Michelin man encourages, because he fails to recognize that the worth of sights is dependent more on the quality of one's vision than on the objects viewed, that there is nothing inherently three-star about a town Proust grew up in or inherently no-star about an Elf petrol station near Courville, where Proust never had a chance to fill a Renault – but where if he had, he might easily have found something to appreciate, for it has a delightful forecourt with daffodils planted in a neat border and an old-fashioned pump which, from a distance, looks like a stout man leaning against a fence wearing a pair of burgundy dungarees.

In the preface to his translation of Ruskin's *Sesame and Lilies*, Proust had written enough to turn the Illiers-Combray tourist industry into an absurdity had anyone bothered to listen:

> We would like to go and see the field that Millet ... shows us in his *Springtime*, we would like Claude Monet to take us to Giverny, on the banks of the Seine, to that bend of the river which he hardly lets us distinguish through the morning mist. Yet in actual fact, it was the mere chance of a connection or family relation that gave ... Millet or Monet occasion to pass or to stay nearby, and to choose to paint that road, that garden, that field, that bend in the river, rather than some other. What makes them appear other and more beautiful than the rest of the world is that they carry on them, like some elusive reflection, the impression they afforded to a genius, and which we might see wandering just as singularly and despotically across the submissive, indifferent face of all the landscapes he may have painted.

It should not be Illiers-Combray that we visit: a genuine homage to Proust would be to look at *our* world through *his* eyes, not look at *his* world through *our* eyes.

To forget this may sadden us unduly. When we feel interest to be so dependent on the exact locations where certain great artists found it, a thousand landscapes and areas of experience will be deprived of possible interest, for Monet only looked at a few stretches of the earth, and Proust's novel, though long, could not comprise more than a fraction of human experience. Rather than learn the general lesson of art's attentiveness, we might seek instead the mere objects of its gaze, and would then be unable to do justice to parts of the world which artists had not considered. As a Proustian idolater, we would have little time for desserts which Proust never tasted, for dresses he never described, nuances of love he didn't cover and cities he didn't visit, suffering instead from an awareness of a gap between our existence and the realm of artistic truth and interest.

*

The moral? That there is no greater homage we could pay Proust than to end up passing the same verdict on him as he passed on Ruskin, namely, that for all its qualities, his work must eventually also prove silly, maniacal, constraining, false and ridiculous to those who spend too long on it.

> To make [reading] into a discipline is to give too large a role to what is only an incitement. Reading is on the threshold of the spiritual life; it can introduce us to it: it does not constitute it.

Even the finest books deserve to be thrown aside.

Acknowledgements

I would like to thank the following: Marie-Pierre Bay, Marina Benjamin, Nigel Chancellor, Jan Dalley, Caroline Dawnay, Dan Frank, Minna Fry, Anthony Gornall, Nicki Kennedy, Ursula Köhler, Jacqueline and Marc Leland, Alison Menzies, Albert Read, Jon Riley, Tanya Stobbs, Peter Straus and Kim Witherspoon. I am particularly indebted to Miriam Gross for her encouragement and a weekly column. For their sharp-eyed proof-reading, I would like to thank Mair and Mike McGeever, Noga Arikha and, as ever, Gilbert and Janet de Botton. My greatest debts are to John Armstrong, for his friendship and two years of extraordinarily insightful conversation; and to Kate McGeever, who endured me throughout the project, and was unfailingly lovely.

Photographic Acknowledgements

Barnaby's Picture Library, 160; Bridgeman Art Library, 20 (Louvre, Paris), 109 (Peter Willi, Musée Marmottan, Paris), 148 (Louvre, Paris/Giraudon), 149 (Louvre, Paris/Giraudon); Mary Evans Picture Library, 45; Hulton Getty Collection, 101a; Simon Marsden, 159